BELIEVE IT!

BECOME IT!

HOW TO HURDLE BARRIERS
AND
EXCEL LIKE NEVER BEFORE

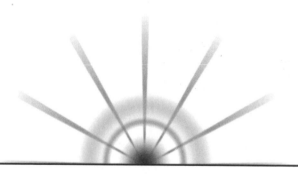

PAULA NOBLE TYLLINGHAM

D1446127

Unlimited Living International, Inc.
P.O. Box 37
Austin, TX 78767

ISBN-10: 0-9705497-2-5

ISBN-13: 978-0-9705497-2-3

Dedication

I dedicate this book to my wonderful parents, Wendell and Gwen Noble, and to extraordinary people everywhere who hurdle enormous barriers and valiantly excel. Their courage to believe it and become it enriches my life and provides inspiration for my writing.

Contents

II. Become

Introduction

The doorbell rang one frosty January morning. It was Mom, standing on the front steps with a grin on her face and a package in her hands. She had found our old Family Time Capsule! You see, on New Years Day 1985, our family wrote goals and placed them in a box we called our Time Capsule. The plan was to review them the following January...but Mom lost the box. Now, years later she was delivering the newly-discovered contents to her grown children. I laughed as I unfolded my yellow-stained notes. My laughter turned to dismay as I read my ancient goals. I could hardly believe my eyes! These goals were nearly identical to the ones I wrote for myself just days before!

Why do we continue setting the same goals for ourselves, year after year?

Believe it and become it. I reveal principles that empower you to hurdle every barrier and excel like never before. When you internalize the *Power Beliefs*, apply the *Success Strategies*, and use the *Daily Action Plan*, you'll improve and enrich your life in ways you never imagined.

In this book you'll learn ways to create positive change and release yourself from negative thoughts...allowing you to rise above life's obstacles and live beyond their energy-sapping, joy-sucking grip. You'll learn how to reflect joy and confidence in your self-mirror; to create your own happiness *and* light the way for others. Then, as you work toward your goals using positive experiencing and positive crisis, you'll understand exactly how to exceed your highest expectations. And finally, through partnering, preparation, and performance you can become your best self and create an extraordinary life.

This is a book for doers. It is a life-changing program for those who want to thrive, not simply survive. If you read this book thoughtfully, and carefully absorb its teachings, then conscientiously practice its principles, you can experience powerful, personal improvement. By using the *5 Pillar Principles* you can modify or change the circumstances in which you now live and take control of them rather than be directed by them. Each of your relationships will improve, and you will have increased influence over everyone in your life's circle. You will enjoy a delightful new sense of well-being, and even increased health. How can I say with certainty that these are the by-products of learning and living the Believe It! BECOME IT! principles? Because I've witnessed amazing results in people's lives and know these concepts are life-changing.

I invite everyone who wants to live joyfully to join me in the adventure of **becoming** our ideal selves.

The first step? Believe.

1

POWER BELIEFS: AN OVERVIEW

"The greatest discovery of my generation is that human beings can alter their lives by altering their beliefs."
William James

Wouldn't it be thrilling to hurdle every barrier in your life and excel like you've never excelled before? You absolutely can! The first step is *believing* that it's possible.

Within each one of us there is a power we scarcely tap. This power has fueled heroic deeds since time began and has energized great inventors, artists and musicians throughout the ages. It's the exact same power available to you every day of your life. It is the power of belief.

What is a belief? It is a sense of certainty about something. For example, if you believe you're a good musician you think, "I feel certain that I'm a fine musician." And that sense of certainty helps you channel your skill, creativity, and resources to produce beautiful music. On the other hand, a negative belief works the same way. If you say, "I believe I'm a terrible singer" then your certainty that you sing badly will actually help orchestrate just the right elements needed to produce results that validate your belief.

The aim of Believe It! BECOME IT! is to ignite the marvelous power of positive belief within you. This power can, without question, amplify and enrich every area of your life. As you study and practice the principles in this book, and as you identify and use positive beliefs in your life, you will gain access to a reservoir of energy and inspiration for constructive personal growth, taking you to a whole new level of living.

Marcus Aurelius, a 2nd century philosopher and
Emperor of Rome once said,

"A man's life is what his beliefs make of it."

And Dale Carnegie, author of the book *How To Win
Friends and Influence People* wrote,

**"Believe that you will succeed. Believe it firmly,
and you will then do what is necessary to
bring success about."**

Through the years I've heard, "How can I believe I'll be successful when my past history tells me otherwise? That's a common question asked by people who are wounded by past failures. They've allowed the blows of life and the multiplication of their challenges to produce entrenched self-doubt. Although these good people *want* to believe they can become their ideal selves, they frequently suffer from a deep sense of inadequacy and insecurity. They simply don't trust their ability to make positive changes in their lives. Their damaged hearts don't allow them to believe in themselves, so they settle for something less than true fulfillment.

The Power Beliefs in this book teach you how to control and direct your thoughts in positive ways. As you develop the sense of certainty that positive beliefs provide, you'll be able to accomplish virtually anything, including those things that others think are impossible.

Take a look at some facts about people who believed in themselves and in their special gifts:

- Dr. Seuss's first children's book was rejected by 23 publishers.
- Michelangelo endured 7 long years lying on his back on a scaffold to paint the Sistine Chapel. He was nearly blinded by the paint that dripped in his eyes.
- Michael Jordan was cut from his high school basketball team.
- Walt Disney went bankrupt four times before he succeeded.
- Charles Goodyear was imprisoned for debt and ridiculed by family and friends.
- Albert Einstein's doctoral dissertation was rejected and called "irrelevant."
- Cyrus Curtis lost over $800,000 on the *Saturday Evening Post* before it realized a single dollar profit.
- Thomas Edison failed one thousand nine hundred ninety-nine times before his invention of the light bulb worked. He remarked, "I am not discouraged because every wrong attempt discarded is another step forward."

I believe we're all here to contribute something unique, and that each of us has a special gift, a particular talent, to share with others.

My hope is that you will come to believe that you don't have to be defeated by anything. You can enjoy peace of mind, boundless energy, compelling confidence and even improved health each and every day of a joy-filled life.

Too many people go through life in quiet unhappiness, defeated by everyday problems. They struggle through their days and nights without knowing that it doesn't have to be that way! Yes, life throws us curves and challenges—frequently. But allowing ourselves to be defeated by difficulties is needless and avoidable. While not ignoring the obstacles and tragedies in our lives, we shouldn't allow them to dominate our minds because the beliefs in our minds create the results in our lives.

As you sow in your mind, so shall you reap in your life. Think of your mind as a bed of rich soil that will help all kinds of seeds to flourish, whether good or bad. If you sow noxious thistles you can't expect to reap luscious fruit. It is essential to allow only good thoughts to grow in the fertile soil of your mind because happiness is directly related to our ability to fill our minds with positive thoughts.

> Whatsoever things are true, whatsoever things are honest, whatsoever things are just, whatsoever things are pure, whatsoever things are lovely, whatsoever things are of good report; if there be any virtue, and if there be any praise, *think on these things.* (Phil. 4:8) For, as *a man thinketh, so is he.*

The World Within Creates the World Without

Another way to explain this concept is that the world *within* creates the world *without*. If you want to change external conditions you must first change the cause...your thoughts. Every thought is a cause, and every condition is an effect. Often, people try to change circumstances by working on the circumstances. Why? Because they fail to see that to remove limitation and lack from your life you must first remove the beliefs and images which encourage that limitation and lack. Change the cause and you change the effect. You possess all the power necessary to heal a troubled mind and a broken heart, and to move forward joyfully. Indeed, you can choose to make your life greater, richer, nobler and better than ever before, or you can choose to live in emotional bondage, in a stagnant or even regressive state.

Let's talk about *how* to create positive change and move forward joyfully.

If we want to make use of physical forces of nature, such as in chemistry, mathematics, and physics, we must first learn the principles. Likewise, if we want to make use of the force of our mind, we must learn its principles.

One law of your mind is this: the response you get from your subconscious mind is determined by the nature of the thoughts in your conscious mind. The latter is like the captain of a ship. He sends orders to people in the engine room who control the ship navigational instruments. The engine room people are like the subconscious mind. They don't know where they're going, they just follow orders. They'd hit rocks and wreck the ship if the captain sent them faulty instructions. Because the captain (conscious mind) is in charge, the engine room people don't talk back to the captain, they just carry out his orders because he's supposed to know what he's doing.

Your conscious mind—the captain of your ship—gives your subconscious mind orders based on your self-beliefs. Then your subconscious mind acts on the orders, without questioning them, even if those beliefs are wrong.

For example, if you say to yourself, "*I'm no good at selling. Hey, I like people, but I just can't sell.*" Then your subconscious mind acts on that belief and will be sure that you don't succeed as a salesman. You will not be able to sell, and you'll believe that circumstances caused it. The fact is, you created your circumstances through your negative belief. Your false belief was the cause, your failure as a salesperson is the effect.

Conscious and Subconscious

You may know that the conscious and subconscious are two spheres of activity within your mind. Your conscious mind reasons and chooses. For example, your decisions like the home you live in, the food you eat, the people you choose as your friends—these choices are made with the conscious mind.

On the other hand, your subconscious mind functions without any conscious choice on your part. It keeps your heart beating automatically and your body functioning without thought. Your subconscious mind doesn't reason things out, it doesn't argue with you, it just blindly accepts your conscious belief, both good and bad. Again, it's like rich soil that accepts any kind of seeds. For example, if you consciously believe something is right—

even if it's wrong—your subconscious mind accepts it as right and then works to make that information correct. It will bring information and suggestions (even the wrong ones) to pass as conditions and experiences. This works for both good and bad like this: When you think, *"I believe I'm a loving, kind person,"* each day you act in loving, kind ways. On the other hand, if you think, *"I'm always impatient with my children,"* you continue to be impatient.

Whatever the conscious, reasoning mind *believes*, the subconscious mind *accepts* and *acts* on.

Your subconscious mind is always working, night and day. It keeps your body functioning even though you aren't consciously participating; it's always on the job for you. Since you can't interact with the subconscious mind, realize that your business is with the conscious mind. Therefore, it is imperative to a healthy, joyful life to sow the seeds of positive thought, gratitude, abundance, love, and peace. Expect the best continuously and fill your mind with goodness. Take care of your conscious mind, knowing that your subconscious mind is always expressing and manifesting according to your habitual thinking.

Almost everything that has happened to you in your life happened because of your conscious beliefs, impressed on your subconscious mind. If you've communicated wrong or distorted beliefs to your subconscious mind, it is urgently important that you correct them. And as you learn new ways of thinking, your subconscious mind will accept your new, healthy thought patterns and they'll become habitual. Your subconscious mind drives habits.

Thinking Patterns Create Deep Grooves

Your habitual thinking patterns create deep grooves in your subconscious mind. If your habitual thoughts are constructive, peaceful, loving, your subconscious mind will respond by creating positive, peaceful, loving conditions in your life. On the other hand, if your thought patterns are fearful, worrisome or otherwise destructive, the good news is that you can use the Power Beliefs to break the cycle and create new, healthy thought habits.

I absolutely know that we have the power to take control and change nearly anything and everything in our lives, because within each of us lies both the ability to turn our dreams into reality, and the solutions to our every challenge.

Deep inside all of us lies the belief that our life experience can be greater than it is. We *want* to raise our standards to a new, more exciting level and to also lift others.

This book is meant to be a powerful personal catalyst. It can help you produce specific, measurable, long-lasting changes. The five Pillar Principles will catapult you forward, allowing you to take giant leaps toward becoming your ideal self. These principles will take you from merely wishing you could improve to reaching—and exceeding— each and every goal you've had on your New Year's resolution list for years.

The 5 Pillar Principles:

1. Power Beliefs
2. Positive Crisis
3. Partnering
4. Preparation
5. Performance

POWER BELIEFS

PARTNERING   PREPARATION

POSITIVE
CRISIS   PERFORMANCE

BELIEVE IT! BECOME IT!

HOW TO HURDLE BARRIERS
AND
EXCEL LIKE NEVER BEFORE

"I'm wealthy beyond my wildest dreams!
Unfortunately, my dreams were never very wild."

2

I CAN CREATE CHANGE

"If we don't change direction soon, we'll end up where we're going."

Irwin Corey

I Choose My Thoughts, Words and Actions

The first step to **becoming** is to get yourself out of the way.

Michael despised his cubicle. He was envious each morning as he passed the offices with doors, occupied by executives behind large mahogany desks. Michael wanted a promotion, but it was a wish, not a goal. A wish is a goal without the do and the deadline.

One evening Michael expressed his discontent to his wife. She quickly reminded him that he should be grateful for his job and be content. "Don't make waves," his wife counseled. "We're fine the way things are. Don't do anything that might put your job at risk!"

The next day Michael repeated her words in his mind as he walked by the executive offices. And he thought, "She's right. I'm not smart enough to get promoted, anyway."

What if Michael had taken another path in his mind? Instead of going down the low road of Negative Thought, he could be striding confidently along the high road of Positive Belief that always leads to successful **becoming.**

You have a myriad of choices every moment, and your mind will take you wherever you wish. The very first and most important thing you need to understand is your role in creating the results that are your life.

Zig Ziglar remarked, "You are free to choose, but the choices you make today will determine what you will have, be, and do in the tomorrow of your life." Indeed, our lives are a sum total of the choices we make.

You Create Your Life with the Choices You Make Each Day

This isn't always what we want to admit, because frequently our choices lead to negative results. But the truth is: we own our lives. Whether we're happy, unhappy, successful or unsuccessful, we're accountable for our choices.

Admittedly, many people are weighed down with challenges that are absolutely no fault of their own. Children are abused, parents divorce, fat genes are part of life, and bad things happen to good people. But right now, as adults, we have choices regarding how we deal with our past and present circumstances. We can either point fingers, blame, withdraw, resent, or we can turn our faces to the future and focus on solutions. We can allow ourselves to be pulled backwards, or we can "take the best and discard the rest" from past experiences, and move forward. The choice is ours.

> *An event may be crucial in the short term, but researchers find that people's enduring self-concept—their view of who they are and what they are capable of—is not tied to any single positive or negative event. Instead, a self-concept is composed of a combination of beliefs and feelings based on long-term experiences both at home and at work (Black, 1999).*

When you choose to resist or deny ownership for your life and for your choices, you also choose stagnation, because as long as you're convinced that you're a victim, you simply cannot begin to heal and progress. If you truly want to improve your life then you must embrace the principle of choice and accountability. This is about taking responsibility for your thoughts, words, and actions. This wonderful principle has the power to set you free from damaging beliefs about yourself and others who may have hurt you. It has the power to release people from all negative habits. As you practice this principle you learn how to live above everything that attempts to pull you down or backwards. So let's learn how to harness the power this principle provides.

The First Power Belief, **"I Can Create Change,"** has three parts:

First, assess where you are in your belief patterns; how you habitually think about yourself, others and your circumstances.

Second, understand the principle of choice. This principle makes change possible.

Third, learn how to release yourself from damaging beliefs by controlling and directing your thoughts.

Assess Your Belief Patterns

Honestly answer these twelve questions:

1. Do I usually think positive thoughts about myself and others?
2. Do I think I'm fairly attractive?
3. Am I usually clever in social situations?
4. Do most of the people in my life's circle like me?
5. Am I kind to my family members?
6. Does my family know that I love them?
7. Am I assertive when I need to be?
8. Do I usually make wise choices about most things in life?
9. Am I generally happy with my home and neighborhood?
10. On most days do I like my job?
11. When I help others do I do it cheerfully?
12. Do I look to the future with optimism?

How did you do? Were most of your answers "no" or "yes?" On one end of the scale are those who answered every question with a "yes." You are usually kind, optimistic people with healthy self-confidence. Your belief patterns are consistently positive and you'll easily handle the second and third parts of this Power Belief. On the other end of the scale are those who answered every question with a "no." In parts two and three of this Power Belief you'll discover ways to lift yourself to a higher, happier level of living.

Most people answered some questions "no" and some "yes." For you, portions of the next two parts will come easily and, using the Daily Action Plan, you'll quickly release yourself from damaging beliefs as you learn how to control and direct your thoughts.

The Principle of Choice Makes Change Possible

I remember the very moment it happened. It was one of those life-altering experiences we often describe as "ah-ha moments," when the mind suddenly seems to expand with new understanding. I was attending a seminar on strengthening relationships, and the speaker quoted Eleanor Roosevelt. That great lady said, **"No one can make me feel inferior without my consent."** I remember thinking, *Wow! That means that we allow people to offend us; we allow people to make us angry. Our reaction to people and our circumstances is our choice!* And then my mind took it a step further and I thought, *that means that if we can allow people to make us angry, we can refuse to be offended or angry!*

Time actually seemed to stand still as I pondered, then

understood, this incredible concept: **We can respond to others and to our circumstances however we choose.** And I realized that the time had come to take control of my life.

Soon afterwards I learned about Victor Frankl. Let me take you to the place where he learned this same priceless lesson:

Victor Frankl Story

The year is 1945. You are in Auschwitz, Germany, imprisoned in a concentration camp whose horror defies description. Your entire family has been killed. You're a Jewish psychiatrist named Viktor Frankl. The guards have stripped you, beaten you, starved you, and deprived you of sleep. And yet you live on, determined to somehow create meaning out of this horror.

As you are experiencing this hell on earth you come to an incredible understanding. The guards can torture you, but you have the power to respond to them however you *choose*. They can beat you, but they can't take away your will to live. They can strip you, but you can clothe yourself with mental power beyond their reach. They can starve you, but you can feast on your dreams of the future. You see, Victor Frankl imagined himself at a university pulpit, teaching the future generation about the ultimate freedom—the freedom to choose how you respond to life. He was passionate about living to tell his story so that never again would a human being be allowed to cause such suffering as he had endured.

Those prison guards couldn't make Victor Frankl angry or discouraged. Think how our lives would change if we truly understood and applied this concept! We would no longer blame others. We wouldn't say, "You make me angry!" because we'd understand that no one *makes* us angry; we can choose to be in control of our emotions. We would no longer blame other people, our circumstances, the weather, etc. for anything. We wouldn't say, "I can't get up that early —I'm just not a morning person!" because we're any kind of a person we choose to be. We wouldn't say, "I'm in a bad mood because the boss is being a jerk today." Or, "My kids are making me crazy!" Do you see how it works?

> *Researchers find that an optimistic personal outlook is more than just seeing the bright side of things. Believing in yourself actually produces increases in good health, motivation, and achievement for six in ten people (Schulman, 1999).*

This is an incredibly important principle. This means that you and you alone own your thoughts, feelings, words, and actions. Is this difficult? Yes, because it's easier when you can point to someone else while you're saying, "It's not my fault—he made me do it!"

This is a wonderful, liberating principle with monumental significance as it relates to personal progress.

"I Choose My Thoughts, Words, and Actions" is part of the first Power Belief because it's the key to personal growth. You must take responsibility for your thoughts, words, and actions if you are to move forward in your life. It is imperative that you understand this principle thoroughly in order to progress. To help you do that, here are three stories of people who do *not* get it.

Marlene and David Didn't Get It

Marlene was furious at David, her husband. It was 7:30 at night and he still wasn't home. She had made a lovely dinner and had prepared his favorite dessert. Marlene and both children had waited until 7:00 o'clock, but they finally gave up and ate without him. With each passing minute Marlene became angrier. She complained to the children about their father's irresponsibility, and after dinner she impatiently paced the floor. When David finally arrived, Marlene exploded with a flood of accusations and belittling remarks.

Was Marlene's behavior justified? Maybe David had promised to be home at 6:00 pm and this was the fourteen time he was late. Maybe it was the first time he was late. That doesn't matter. The question is, should David's behavior determine Marlene's reaction?

If Marlene understood that we are responsible for our emotions, regardless of the words or actions of others, perhaps she would have handled it differently. Her children certainly would have learned a far different lesson that night. This is how the evening might have looked if Marlene didn't blame David:

Marlene thought, *Darn, David is late again. I wonder what happened. I hope this dessert will taste as good when he gets home.* "Well, kids," she remarked cheerfully, "It looks like Dad won't be here for dinner, but look how delicious this looks! Hop up to the table and let's eat." Then instead of focusing on David and the possible reasons for why he wasn't there, Marlene focused on the children. She asked each one about what they learned at school that day, she shared her experiences of the day, and she genuinely enjoyed the meal. After dinner Marlene read stories to the children.

Does understanding this principle mean that we never get upset when things go wrong? Of course not. The difference is that we don't blame others for our reactions. We learn how to control our emotions and we wait until an appropriate time to discuss the problem. And when the time comes to talk about it we communicate in a way that doesn't create more problems.

Another unhealthy scenario occurs when people choose not to *say* anything, but instead harbor negative, critical *thoughts*.

A Lesson Learned

Joseph and his wife Sharon love their family, and stay in close touch with their children and their grandchildren. When their daughter, Jody, began having marital problems, they were concerned and supported her the best way they knew how. After her divorce, she began dating heavily and brought her two young children to Grandpa and Grandma's house often. Joseph and Sharon wanted Jody to be happy; but as time went on, they felt more and more used. They began resenting the grandchildren and became angry with their daughter. However, they didn't say anything to her and continued to watch the children each time she asked because they were afraid she'd be upset.

How would Joseph and Sharon handle this situation if they understood that 1) when we allow someone to make

us a victim, it's our choice, and 2) we're all responsible for
our thoughts, words and actions?

As soon as Jody began bringing her children too often,
Joseph and Sharon could have started a calm discussion
with their daughter. "Jody, we love you and want you to
be happy, but we're not comfortable tending the children
as often as you want us to. We'll be glad to watch them
one evening each week." Then (and this is important)
Joseph and Sharon would likely begin to think more kindly
about their daughter and grandchildren. If unkind
thoughts crept in, they would label them as such and work
on replacing them.

Does this take mental strength? Yes. Can it be done?
Absolutely! Let's examine one more example:

Two Endings to the Story

Diane thought she should be promoted at work. She
was qualified, worked hard, and did everything she was
asked to do. However, when promotions were announced,
Diane was overlooked and Steven got the job she wanted.
Diane told every co-worker, "I am *way* more qualified
than Steven, and I've been here longer!" She repeated her
disapproval for weeks. Then she began coming late to work,
and not giving 100% effort when she was there. "Well,"
Diane reasoned, "Why should I do my best when it doesn't
make any difference? If those executives had given me the
promotion, I would've been great. It's their fault I'm turning in lousy work."

If Diane understood, and took responsibility for her
thoughts, words, and actions, her behavior may have been
far different:

When she heard the news that Steve got the promotion, Diane could have swallowed her pride and congratulated him. Although she may have been disappointed, she would have understood that it wasn't Steve's fault, or the executive's fault. *"You know,"* Diane may have thought, *"There must be a bigger picture that I don't see. Oh well, there will be other promotions, and I'm going to work really hard to qualify for the next one!"*

But You Don't Understand!

As you read those examples, you may think, *"You don't understand! I have some real challenges in my life. And there are genuine toxic personalities I have to deal with on a daily basis! It's really NOT my fault that my life is the way it is. It's my parent's fault—or my wife's fault—or my boss' fault."*

OK, let's go there.

First, let me console you by saying that it is at the very core of human nature to blame other people. It's like "survival of the fittest"—self-preservation—to try to escape accountability. You don't want to be responsible, because if you are, you're accountable. Then you have to experience the consequences of your mistakes, *every* time. You're where the buck stops.

It's far more difficult to accept accountability for your life. But once you "get it" and grab hold—taking responsibility for the results in your life—you'll begin achieving as you've *never* achieved before. If you truly want to progress, you must go to work and take control of every part of your life.

However, let me be very clear: Until you stop blaming others for your problems; until you stop convincing yourself that you are a victim, you will never progress. You will remain in a backwards-focus, finger-pointing mode that spells f-a-i-l-u-r-e. No growth. No achievement. No extraordinary life.

On a plaque that hung in Mother Teresa's Calcutta orphanage, Kent Keith wrote the following words:

> *People are often unreasonable and self-centered,*
> Forgive them anyway.
>
> *If you are kind, people may accuse*
> *you of ulterior motives.*
> Be kind anyway.
>
> *If you are honest, people may cheat you.*
> Be honest anyway.
>
> *If you find happiness, people may be jealous.*
> Be happy anyway.
>
> *The good you do today may be forgotten tomorrow.*
> Do good anyway.
>
> *Give the world the best you have,*
> *and it may never be enough.*
> Give your best anyway.
>
> *For you see, in the end, it is between you and God.*
> It was never between you and them anyway.

To Move Forward, Embrace This

To move forward with your life you must fully embrace the fact that the solutions to nearly every one of your life's challenges lie within you.

Remember the examples above? Since Marlene understands that she creates her own results, she doesn't believe that her husband's behavior justifies her losing control; so she chooses to focus on enjoying the meal and her children.

If Joseph and Sharon accept accountability for their lives, they'll take control of the situation as soon as it becomes uncomfortable for them, and create a positive solution.

When Diane accepts accountability for her life, she is then able to take her loss in stride, with graciousness and dignity. She can move forward, free of anger and envy—those unpleasant "companions" of people who don't accept responsibility for the results in their lives.

You may believe that something in your childhood, which was far beyond your control, caused you pain and that's why you are troubled.

How about the little girl who was raped, or the little boy who was molested? How can they possibly "create their own results?" People who have had their childhoods stolen, for any reason, often feel that since they were wronged, they aren't accountable for their own behavior as adults.

No one will disagree that intentionally hurting children is a grievous sin. The adults who cause such pain are depraved and should be punished. However, you will never fix your problems blaming someone else. When you were a child, you didn't have the power to choose the events in your life; but things have changed, and you are an adult, now. As an adult, you <u>can</u> choose your reaction to those childhood events and circumstances. To move past the past, you must understand that in the todays and tomorrows of your life you can gain control by accepting responsibility for your thoughts, words, and actions.

Relative to unfortunate events in your past, you have choices. You can re-live them, focusing backwards with a pointed finger. Or you can face forward, replacing past sadness with **positive beliefs** about who you are now, and with **positive goals** to create the successful person you'll be tomorrow. The choice is yours. I'm guessing that since you're reading this book, you've already made the right choice. Let's move on to *how* to replace past sadness and damaging beliefs with positive ones. Later, we'll talk about those positive goals.

Release Yourself from Damaging Beliefs

We each carry with us mental pictures of ourselves; our "self beliefs." These beliefs may be unclear to our conscious mind, but they're there, down to the last detail. They are our ideas about who we are, formed from past experiences, successes and failures, embarrassing moments, achievements, (both big and small), and the way people have treated us, especially during childhood. From all these experiences, we mentally create pictures of ourselves. Once a belief about ourselves goes into this picture, it becomes a "fact" to us and we don't question its validity; we act as though it were true.

Your self beliefs form the foundation for your personality and your behavior. Therefore, these self beliefs are the key to change. This is true for two reasons: First, your actions are always consistent with your beliefs. Second, your beliefs *can* be changed.

Simply stated, **we act like the person we believe ourselves to be.** We literally cannot act otherwise, in spite of our conscious efforts. Because our actions are always in harmony with our beliefs, ideas which are inconsistent with our beliefs are rejected (by our subconscious minds), not believed, and therefore not acted upon.

It should be clear, then, only ideas that are consistent with our core beliefs will be accepted and acted upon.

Dr. Maxwell Maltz , author of *Psycho-Cybernetics*, underscored this when he wrote: "The man who conceives himself to be a 'failure type person' will find some way to fail, in spite of all his good intentions, or his will power, even if opportunity is literally dumped in his lap. The person who conceives himself to be a victim of injustice, one 'who was meant to suffer,' will invariably find circumstances to verify his opinions."

Unfortunately, many people are told, when they're young, that they're failures in some area. Parents say things like, "You'll never excel in math because none of our family can figure it out! We just don't understand it!" Other parents make similar comments regarding music, athletics, etc. Remember back to your own childhood. Did anyone ever tell you that you weren't a good singer, or that you couldn't draw well? Or perhaps you were told that you'd never be a good basketball player, and so on. Most adults can easily remember stinging comments like these.

Children who hear such remarks, day after day, soon come to believe them. They create negative self-talk (how we talk to ourselves in our minds). They think, *"I'm just no good in math, none of my family is."* Or, *"I could never make the team, so I just won't try out."* Or, *"Since I can't sing, I shouldn't take chorus, and I'd make a fool of myself if I tried out for the school musical."* Then, sure enough, these same children don't excel in those areas, and usually their report cards verify their beliefs. Children then have "proof" that they're failures. And because of this objective "proof," they don't question their incompetence. Sadly, *these young people don't ever think that the trouble may lie in their own beliefs about themselves.* And yet, tell a young person who is failing in math that he only "thinks" he can't understand it and he won't believe you! He's tried and tried, and still his report card tells the story. Often he gets a low score on a test, and instead of saying, "I failed that test," he'll think to himself, *"Yep, I'm a failure!"*

And perhaps the saddest fact of all is that we carry these negative beliefs throughout our lives! We develop limiting beliefs about who we are and what we're capable of from our earliest years, then we carry those negative self beliefs for decades. Based on past failures, we believe we'll fail in the future. But the wonderful news is—*the past doesn't equal the future*!

How about the businesswoman who believes she can't sell? Oh, she'll agree that she has good people-skills; she's friendly and personable. But this woman was rejected by the first six people to whom she tried to sell a product, and now firmly believes she'll never be a good salesperson. "I'm just not good at it," she'll explain. Additionally, she believes that she will never earn more than a certain figure, and her paycheck proves it month after month. And sometimes, instead of saying, "I'm not a good salesperson," she says, "I'm a failure." And then she allows her failure in one area to affect other areas of her life.

Our life experiences confirm, and thereby strengthen, our self beliefs, and positive or negative cycles are created.

Most of us recognize that we have a few negative self beliefs that impede our progress and personal growth in some areas. But the good news is that negative self beliefs can be changed! We're never too young or too old to reverse our negative beliefs and start living a life full of extraordinary achievements!

More Than Positive Thinking

What we're talking about is more than "positive thinking," however. This is about changing your core self beliefs. It's not about someone gritting his teeth and thinking, "I *will* make this sale!" Rather, thoughts about 'self' are altered. He thinks, "I am a successful salesman. In fact, I do quite well at most things!" Pessimistic, harmful core beliefs need to be fundamentally changed into positive ones.

Dr. Maltz wrote, **"It is literally impossible to really think positively about a particular situation as long as you hold a negative concept of self. And numerous experiments have shown that once the concept of self is changed, other things consistent with the new concept of self are accomplished easily and without strain."**

When you change your negative self-beliefs, that underlie all of your negative actions, you increase your ability to act in positive ways. Then, achieving your goals —in every area of your life—becomes easier and easier.

Let's get real clarity about a few points we've discussed:

1. You are who you are because of the dominating thoughts you permit in your mind.

2. You can either choose to attack yourself with negativity or affirm your abilities.

3. Positive mental picturing is a key to healthy change. You are the writer, director and star of either an Oscar-winning epic (an extraordinary life) or a Grade 'B' movie (less than your best). The person you see in your imagination will always rule your world.

The key is you. You must:

- Believe you can change, and *want* to change your negative self-beliefs
- Identify the beliefs you need to alter
- Learn and use key skills

Believe You Can Change Your Negative Self-beliefs

To take control in any area of your life, the very first step is to create a belief that says with certainty, "I can do this!" When you develop this sense of certainty, you can accomplish virtually anything.

People develop this certainty in different ways. Some people take the first step and realize on their own (before life becomes painful) that change is not only possible, but highly desirable. Other people have family and friends who lovingly point out the need for change, and encourage them in positive directions. Still others don't have a support system; they "go it alone." Then, when the pain becomes too great, they find the courage within to change. Many look to God for additional strength to move forward and break the cycle of negativity or destruction in their lives.

Those who struggle to believe they *can* change their negative self-beliefs, and develop a powerful sense of certainty, may be encouraged by those who hurdled similar barriers.

Tawni, from Utah, desperately tried to overcome her negative feelings. She shares her story:

> I had absolute terror panic attacks which would render me completely sleepless and immobile. This fear would drive my decisions

about activities, travel, work, etc. What got me through it? The number one thing was my desire. Down to my toes I desired to be free! I'm now 46 years old, and it took approximately 44 years to achieve, but I'm here! The second "help" was *my total belief* that God would help me conquer. Third, were friends, and learning about kinesiology. I learned about how the brain/body is organized and balanced. I worked hard, and eventually my old patterns of fear went out and I put calm, new ones in. My advice to others who want to accomplish this is to *believe it can be done*, trust God, and get educated about your problem. Celebrate your baby step improvements. I can now stay alone, travel alone, and I think completely differently. I am finally free!

Sara, age 23, from California, described her struggles and accomplishment:

Since childhood I have been a compulsive overeater. It was the compulsive overeating combined with depression and extremely low self esteem that led to my eating disorder of Bulima Nervousa. I was bulimic every day for almost two years during my college years. It was then I became completely powerless over binge vomiting. It was something I could not give up. I would wake up in the morning praying for the strength to make it just one day without binging or vomiting, and by lunch time I had already succumbed to the disease. Every day was a struggle to survive. After seeking professional help, I was led to Overeaters Anonymous (OA) and *they helped me believe* I could do this. I became abstinent after two weeks of attending the program. I relapsed six months later but was able to regain abstinence. It has been nearly three years since I've been in recovery.

The answer for me was *believing I could change*, sharing my thoughts and feelings at the OA meetings, and being accepted unconditionally. They knew how to cure my unbelieving heart. Also, picking up the phone and talking to others brought my despairing mind back to reality. Another thing that helped me is service. Doing charitable acts of kindness for others always helped me feel better. Lastly, journal writing, reading good books, and praying have been things I've done to get me through the hard times.

My advice to others is to not give up, no matter what. You may slip and fall and feel like your troubles will never end, but "this too shall pass." One day at a time is all you have to get through. *Begin by believing you can do it.*

One of my heroes, the ever-positive Walt Disney, once said, "When you believe in a thing, believe in it all the way, implicitly and unquestionably." I would like to urge you to believe in your power and ability to change; believe you can turn from negativity and from every damaging belief that pulls you backwards; believe you can replace harmful beliefs with new, positive ones that will catapult you forward to exhilarating success.

Identify the Beliefs You Need to Alter

To begin any change, first you need to identify all behaviors needing change, because you can't alter what you don't acknowledge. And if you refuse to acknowledge your own self-destructive beliefs and behaviors, not only will they continue, they'll become more deeply entrenched and grow more resistant to change.

Acknowledgement of your weaknesses (and strengths) requires absolute honesty about what is and what isn't working in your life. You need to know both what's working, (which you can *celebrate*) and what's not, so you can fix it.

I offer an exercise that will help you identify the beliefs you need to alter. However, before we begin:

- First, give yourself permission to examine and question every belief you now hold about yourself.
- Second, open your mind to the possibility that some of your beliefs—even ones you've firmly held as true—may be false.
- Third, allow the possibility that some of your beliefs may be preventing you from moving forward as you'd like.

Now, we're ready for the exercise. Relax and take an unhurried few moments to answer the questions below (simply reflect on your responses to each question; nothing need be written down for this exercise).

1. Name the person or people who bring you the greatest joy. Think about why they make you happy.
2. Name the thing you most enjoy doing. Think about how you feel when you're doing it.

3. Name a place you love to go. Think about that place and, using your imagination, "go there" for a few moments.

4. Now, name a person in your life who causes you sadness and pain.

5. Name what you like least about your job or about your family.

6. Think about a time when someone you care about humiliated or deeply hurt you.

If you did that exercise thoughtfully, taking your time and imagining in great detail, you experienced the marvelous power of the mind. In a matter of seconds, you can go from happiness and peace to agitation and discomfort, even anger. This same mind power will be your ally as you attempt to identify the negative behaviors in your life that need altering. As you carefully question your self-beliefs, in your heart of hearts, you will know what needs correcting in your life.

And, with that same mind power, you can control your thoughts—if you choose. There are three steps. Each one is mandatory, if you are to successfully control your thoughts.

1. **LABEL**

2. **REPLACE**

3. **FOCUS FORWARD**

Label Your Negative Thoughts

Labeling your negative thoughts is like casting a light into a dark room—it disperses the darkness (negativity). Labeling is the critical part of this solution because when a negative thought enters your mind, you can either pay attention and stop it—by labeling it immediately—or you can let your mind take you along a negative path and allow the thought to grow and fester. A far better choice is to "nip it in the bud." This requires you to exert some willpower and strength of character. The very moment a negative thought enters your mind, label it with something like:

- "That was negative."
- "That was unkind." (Name the thought: critical, judgmental, etc.)
- "That wasn't like me. I usually don't think negative thoughts."

The third comment (above) is a superb self-fulfilling prophecy that helps people hurdle the barrier of habitually negative thought patterns.

Replace Your Negative Thoughts

Replacing negative thoughts is most effectively done by trying to 'be' the person you're thinking about, with their needs and life experiences. This requires you to put yourself in the other person's position and really consider why he's speaking or acting as he is. Most of the time, with this perspective, even if you don't agree with the person, at least you can replace the negative thought with something like:

- "I can understand why she's doing (saying) that. It's because she…"
- "If I understood her better, I'd probably like her more. I'll get to know her."
- "Too bad he acts (talks) that way. What can I learn from it?"
- "Different strokes for different folks!"

Focus Your Thinking Forward

Healthy forward thinking is the third step. Instead of focusing backwards, blaming others, or wallowing in negativity, fill your mind with positive thoughts that move you forward. Is it always easy? No. Is it possible? Absolutely! Does it sometimes take creativity? You bet. Here are some examples of positive, forward thinking that are solution-based:

- "I usually don't think unkind thoughts like that. I'll do better next time."
- "Tomorrow will be better. Good days usually follow rough ones!"
- "I might not have all the facts. I'll learn more and it'll probably make sense."

And this is perfect for adults who regret any past action:

- "I made the best decision I could with the information I had at the time. I have more information now, and I'll do better in the future."

The steps to change negative self-beliefs aren't difficult. But, as with all things worth doing, the process requires effort. And yet, don't let yourself become discouraged if you have trouble in the beginning, if changing your thought patterns proves to be difficult for you. Your previous ways of thinking are habits and **it takes about three to six weeks to break a habit.** Have the courage to keep trying until you naturally and easily think predominantly positive thoughts.

It comes back to the question, "How badly do you really want to change?" And that reminds me of a well-known story about Socrates.

What The Seeker Needs

One afternoon, a young man approached Socrates, the wise old philosopher, and exclaimed, "Socrates, I want to know what you know! I want knowledge and wisdom like yours!" The gentle Socrates replied, "Very well, young man. Follow me." And he led the youth to a nearby pond, where he held the boy's head under the water for quite a long time. When Socrates finally released his grip, the young man jerked up out of the water and gasped, "Socrates! Why did you do that?" The philosopher calmly asked, "Young man, when you were under the water, what did you want most in the world?" The boy answered, "Air! I wanted air!" And then Socrates patiently explained, "Young man, when you want knowledge and wisdom as badly as you wanted air, you'll find a way to get it."

I would like to submit that when your desire for change and improvement is great enough, you'll make the effort to control your thoughts and direct them in positive ways.

We'll conclude this Power Belief the way we began—by assessing your self beliefs in an attempt to ascertain the positive ones that empower and strengthen you, and the negative ones that limit you. You'll keep the first and discard the second.

This is first done by carefully questioning and examining your beliefs. Now take a quality moment of unhurried time—right now—and ask yourself these questions:

Do I have beliefs (that I may have held for years) which might be wrong? What are they?

Now, it's tough to re-examine your core beliefs. It is difficult to scrutinize the personal convictions you've held for years. You're doing this, though, because some of your closely-held beliefs might be preventing you from reaching your goals and becoming your ideal self. Defining and questioning those beliefs is the first step.

To discover your long-held limiting beliefs, ask *why* you either succeed or fail in each of these life areas:

Ask yourself two questions for each area in your life:

- Physical   Do I excel physically? If not, why not?
- Mental
- Social
- Emotional
- Financial
- Spiritual
- With Relationships

Now ask yourself (in each area):

"What positive beliefs can replace my negative ones?"

Here's an example of how to do this:

Physical. *Do I excel?* "No." *Why not?* "Because I was never any good at sports. I was overweight/My parents didn't encourage me/There wasn't an athletic program at my school."

What positive beliefs can replace the negative ones? "Even though I wasn't involved in sports in school, it isn't too late to start learning and getting in shape. I can swim each morning with the community group at the local pool/I can jog around the high school track before work in the mornings, and perhaps join a competitive program for masters when I'm ready/I can join the local work-out facility/I can shoot hoops with my buddies (or children). It's never too late to have fun!"

Another exercise that provides clarity begins with asking yourself the following questions:

> "What will the consequences be (what will happen) if I continue believing as I do?"
>
> "Will those consequences bring me happiness or unhappiness?"
>
> "What would I have to believe in order to succeed and enjoy greater happiness?"

The answers to these questions will most likely be revealing. Remember, one well-known definition of insanity is "doing the same thing over and over, expecting different results." If some part of your life isn't working, question your beliefs and make changes.

Examine each belief that keeps you from being successful—at home, at work, in your relationships, etc. and
replace those negative beliefs with positive ones. Choose
beliefs that empower you and make you a better person.
Release yourself from damaging beliefs. It will take effort
and creativity, but the rewards are unlimited. I suggest
you do this self-discovery exercise with a loved one who
deeply cares about your well-being, and with whom you
are completely comfortable.

> **"Our dilemma is that we hate change and love it
> at the same time; what we want is for things to
> remain the same but get better."**
> *Sydney Harris*

"That's our mission statement. If people follow
that, everything else seems to fall into place."

3

I AM JOYFUL AND CONFIDENT

"Happiness depends upon ourselves."
Aristotle

Think for a moment about the people you most admire in your life. Who are you drawn to? Usually it's the joyful ones who smile, laugh, compliment others and radiate happiness.

I Create My Own Happiness

Happiness is all about focus. Whatever you focus on pulls you in that direction, either negative or positive. So the secret to happiness is to *choose* to focus on the positive in life, no matter what. Abraham Lincoln said, "Folks are about as happy as they make up their minds to be." I'd say President Lincoln was an expert at creating his own happiness, wouldn't you? Time and time again, that amazing man refused to let failure keep him from success.

Clinton, age 35, from Balga, Western Australia, is another extraordinary man. Although stricken with severe cerebral palsy, Clinton shares his joyful heart freely. When asked how he keeps going through the tough times he answered, "I always think positive thoughts, I always have a happy outlook on life, and I always pray to God."

How can we focus on the positive? Exactly what do we think that helps us create happiness? Here are several ideas:

1. **Think *gratitude*.** Instead of looking at what you don't have, pay attention to what you *do* have and to the good things about your life.

    For example, when you begin to think thoughts like, *Man, I wish I had a car like that!* Catch yourself and think, *Hey, no matter how fast his car can go, the speed limit is 65 for all of us! My car is great, and I'm OK.*

    Another one: *She is so gorgeous! I'll never look like her because I was born with a shape like a pear!* Again, stop and think, *I'm so glad I'm healthy. I like my life and every day I'm making it better and better!*

    Dale Carnegie once remarked, "Happiness doesn't depend on outward conditions. It depends on inner conditions. It isn't what we have or who we are, or what we are doing that makes us happy or unhappy. It's what we think about it. For example, two people may be in the same place, doing the same thing, at the same time, and yet one is miserable and the other happy. Why? Because of a different mental attitude." And that attitude is *gratitude.*

Mr. Carnegie would enjoy the results of an experiment completed in Washington D.C. by J. Brebner, in 1995: "Happy people and unhappy people explain the world differently. When an unhappy person must interpret the world, 8 in 10 times he or she will see the negative in an event. When a happy person must interpret the world, 8 in 10 times he or she will see the positive." (12)

That experiment was validated by Teresa, age 39, when she said, "I tried to remove thoughts of being a 'victim' of my circumstances to that of being a 'student.' Every time I felt like a victim, I felt sorry for myself and disempowered. When I was able to shift my perspective to being *grateful for the lessons I was learning*, I was able to shift my mind into feeling positive and hopeful. I believe that pain in life is inevitable, but misery is optional."

I'd like to share a personal experience that significantly affected my level of gratitude. In May, 2001, I attended the annual conference of the World Movement of Mothers, held that year at NATO Headquarters in Brussels, Belgium. This marvelous group of women, organized in 1949, has the distinction

> *People who have experienced similar life events can wind up with nearly opposite perceptions of life satisfaction. Researchers have compared, for example, people who have received a job promotion, and they found that while some of the people treasure the opportunity, others lament the added responsibility. The implications of life events are a matter of perspective (Chen, 1996).*

of being the first non-government organization to influence the policy-making at the United Nations. Their hearts are good and their mission is to honor motherhood and strengthen families worldwide.

At that conference my heart was touched as I listened to stories of women who literally help change the world. The representative from France spoke about character-strengthening classes in their schools. She explained that all French school children learn ethics from their earliest years. Commendable! And the Swedish representative spoke about stay-at-home moms in her country who receive social security when their children are raised. Admirable!

But the woman who changed my perspective forever lives in Mali, West Africa. She courageously stood and described the difficult living conditions in her country. She explained that open sewage runs through her village. And in her village there are dirt floors in the huts, lean-to structures, and caves where they live. What does she do to strengthen families in her country? She buries the dead aids victims and then raises their children. Currently, in her cave, she tenderly nurtures many children.

As I listened, my heart filled with love and empathy for this extraordinary woman, and her story prompted an overwhelming feeling of gratitude for my countless blessings. However, at

> *"Studies find that happy people experience much the same range of events as unhappy people. The real difference is in what they define as positive and negative. Happy people are those who use a lower threshold in order to label an event positive"* (Parducci, 1995).

the same time, I felt ashamed of the many things I take for granted each day of my life. Oh, what a valuable perspective we acquire when we develop an attitude of gratitude!

2. **Offer love and kindness**. We have all seen the magical effects of loving kindness in our lives and in the lives of others. It seems as though the giver is always more blessed than the receiver; for as we love, we are loved and it becomes easier to love.

    Mother Teresa said, "Spread love wherever you go. Give love to your husband, your wife, your children, to your next door neighbor. Let no one ever come to you without leaving better and happier. Be the living expression of God's kindness. Kindness in your eyes, kindness in your smile, kindness in your warm greeting."

    In the book *Heart of Goodness*, JoAnne Larsen tells the story of a young nursing school student who buzzed through a test until she came to the last question, which completely stymied her. The question: "What is the first name of the school's head custodian?" Well, the student didn't know, nor did anyone else. When asked by a classmate whether the last question would count toward their grade, the professor said, "Absolutely!" teaching the class that, as nurses, they would cross paths with people from every walk of life; all of whom had ultimate value. And, thus, all people were worthy of the nurses' utmost care and consideration, even if their efforts consisted of a gesture so small as a smile and a greeting. Describing her experience as a lesson never forgotten, the student relates that she still remembers the custodian's name, which she later learned. It was Dorothy.

I recall Etienne de Grellet's words:

> I shall pass through this life but once.
> Any good, therefore, that I can do or any
> Kindness I can show to any fellow creature,
> Let me do it now.
> Let me not deter or neglect it,
> For I shall not pass this way again.

A final thought on creating joy and confidence, from John Wesley:

> "Do all the good you can, in all the ways you can, to all the souls you can, in every place you can, at all the times you can, and with all the zeal you can, as long as ever you can." (*Heart of Goodness*, 2000, foreword).

3. **Be others-centered,** instead of self-centered. Look through windows, seeing the needs of others, instead of through mirrors, seeing only your own needs.

   This principle is magical. When you focus on others, your problems diminish, you're happier, and well-loved. An old saying is, "All that you send into the lives of others comes back into your own."

   This principle embraces patience, forgiving quickly, serving others gladly, noticing others' needs before your own, and seeking to understand before you try to be understood. These are simple, yet profound "guarantees" for happiness.

   The best way to be others-centered is to treat people the way you'd want them to treat you. Think deeply about the people in your life's circle, one by one. Think about what it would be like to *be* those people, with their life experiences, their needs and desires. For example, at the end of a long, frustrating day - as you're walking in the door of your home and all you can think about

> *"Those who regularly ruminate over negative subjects and unhappiness are 70% less likely to feel content than those who do not"* (Scott and McIntosh, 1999).

is food and relaxation, what if one of your loved ones is upset? Can you immediately put aside all thoughts of self and focus only on that person's concerns? Can you be sincerely compassionate, rather than annoyed at the inconvenience?

God's Little Devotional Book for Leaders (1997), tells of a young man who made great personal sacrifices as he kindly reached out to help strangers.

When Chris Gross of Santa Clara, California, heard about the 137 children who lost at least one parent in the bombing of a federal building in Oklahoma City, he thought, "*Where would I be if my folks weren't around when I was growing up?*" With that motivation, he set up a college fund for those children. His first step was to call the CEO of his company and explain his intentions, and that he would be donating his annual salary as an investment analyst—all $53,874 of it—to the fund. He then challenged his company and eighteen others to match his gift, so that the fund might reach one million dollars. "It's not easy living without a paycheck," Gross admitted, but the 26 year-old had no debts and lived frugally with four roommates.

Word of Gross' sacrificial gift quickly spread through the central coast region of California, and many residents responded with personal gifts. Several benefit shows, concerts and seminars were held, including benefits by the San Francisco Opera and the San Francisco Giants. Can one man make a difference? In four months the fund Gross established grew to $525,000!

Pam, age 59, hurdled her shyness 'barrier' by focusing on others. She explained:

> I overcame extreme shyness and feelings of inferiority that made it almost impossible for me to do anything in front of people such as teach, speak, etc. One of the major things I tried to do was focus on others, their feelings and needs, rather than my discomfort. The more I was able to do this, the more I recognized that no one else really paid attention to how I looked or sounded, they were more concerned with themselves.

> I didn't feel qualified to serve as some others did in large, spectacular ways, but I knew I could do small acts of service and do them consistently. Whenever I felt inferior, I reminded myself that even insignificant acts add up and contribute to the whole.

To evaluate your level of other-centeredness, take a quick three-question quiz and answer in your mind "true or false."

- When someone gives a compliment to another person, it makes me think I'm not as good. (Rejoice with the person; it's no reflection on you)

- I worry that everyone will notice my weight/wrinkles/ baldness.

   (Don't focus on yourself—no one else does!)

- I'm so embarrassed because I'm not a very good com- puter technician /secretary/ teacher. (Your focus shouldn't be on your embarrassment, but rather on how you can improve your skills and thus contribute more).

4. **Be flexible and cheerful.** Choosing to be flexible is choosing to focus on the positive. People who adapt well and who are cheerful, no matter what's happen- ing around them, are appreciated and well-loved. There are many times in our lives when we simply aren't in control of the situation. Our ability to adapt well is an indicator of our strength of character. A saying I learned when I was young is, "Be pretty if you are, be wise if you can, but be cheerful if it kills you!"

Change is an inevitable part of life. We have choices relative to the change going on in our lives – we can be flexible and bend graciously, or we can fight it and be unhappy. Again, these are choices. In retrospect, we usually see even the most jolting of life changes as "cata- lysts" for growth.

What we are talking about here, over and over, really, is simply our attitudes.

> *"People who like what they have are twice as likely to be happy as those who actually have the most"* (Sirgy, Cole, Kosenko and Meadow, 1995).

Roberto De Vicenzo, upon completing a golf tournament, was approached by a woman who stated her daughter had leukemia and pled for money to pay medical bills—money he produced. Later, a friend told De Vivenzo the woman's daughter wasn't ill—she had lied to him. In response, Roberto replied, "The child is well? My friend, that's the best news I ever heard!"

General Dwight D. Eisenhower paid a visit to front-line troops during WWII and braved rain and ankle-deep mud to address the men from a makeshift platform. After finishing, as he turned to go, Eisenhower slipped from the platform and sprawled in the mud, sparking the soldiers to roar with laughter. The commanding major general accompanying Eisenhower helped him to his feet, apologizing profusely for his men's behavior. "It's all right," the President responded. "That fall probably helped their morale much more than my speech!" (Remen, *Heart of Goodness, 2000*).

Cheerfulness is an attitude!

ATTITUDE
By Charles Swindoll

The longer I live the more I realize
the impact of attitude on life.
Attitude to me, is more important than facts,
it is more important than the past, than education,
than money, than circumstances, than failures,
than successes, than what other people think or say or do.
It is more important than appearances, giftedness or skill.
It will make or break a company, a church, a home.
The remarkable thing is we have a choice every day regarding

> the attitude we embrace for that day.
> We cannot change our past, we cannot change the fact
> that people will act in a certain way.
> We cannot change the inevitable.
> The other thing we can do is play on the one string
> we have, and that is our attitude.
> I am convinced that life is 10% what happens to me
> and 90% how I react to it

Michael, age 53, from Elkhart, Indiana, is an extraordinary example of this virtue. At age 16, he was diagnosed with rheumatoid arthritis. This chronic disease progressed and severely affected his hands and feet. It frequently attacks his other joints as well. Daily he suffers excruciating pain and severe loss of function. He cheerfully explained:

> I am, and always have been, an optimist! I also figure that there are some things I cannot control, so I make the best of what I have to work with. I can mope and cry and complain, or I can just say, "This is not going to beat me!" and do what I need/want to do. I choose the latter course. I have been in many medical facilities and I've seen a lot of people in worse condition than I am, so I thank God I can do what I can. My advice to others is to think positively.

Career analysts find that 83 percent of mid-career professionals believe chance played a significant role in their ultimate career path and that they highly value staying open for unexpected opportunities (Williams, Soeprapto, Like, Touradji, Hess, and Hill, 1998).

Pace yourself. Know your physical limits. Ask for
help and don't give up.

5. **Be passionate about something**. People who open
their eyes each morning and immediately look forward to something that they're passionate about are
usually more satisfied, happy, and hopeful people who
focus on the positive. How do we become passionate
about something? We develop it the same way we
develop any virtue—love, kindness, patience—we practice it. Look at your life and find something that you
really enjoy doing. Schedule time in for things you
love doing and make them a priority in your life. You
can give better from your 'overflow,' so fill your cup!

William, age 64, in Dallas, Texas, is deeply passionate
about his work. His story is an example to us all.

One day, William, an experienced designer, was asked
by a client to build a large, elaborate model. It called
for several building interiors and hundreds of human
figures. The model was to be created in a scale of one
inch to five feet, which meant that each of the human
figures was only a little more than an inch in height.
Each one had to be hand-painted, using a brush with
a single hair. As William hunched over his table one
day, painstakingly painting the figures and then carefully gluing them in place, one of his employees asked
him, "Don't you find this tedious?"

The designer replied, "Tedious? My goodness, no!
I've loved making and painting models ever since I
made my first model airplane at age seven. I just can't
believe someone is actually paying me to do this!"

From golfers to professional singers, those who *excel* are passionate about their interest.

From an early age, Larry lived and breathed golf. As a teenager, he was ranked one of the top 16 young golfers in the nation. Then, at the beginning of his senior year of high school, Larry was in an automobile accident. He suffered severe injuries, but the most devastating was that his left arm had to be amputated just below the elbow.

After several months of practice with a prosthetic hand, Larry hit a ball. When it landed more than 200 yards away, he knew he could do it. He rejoined his high school team, scoring even better than before, and was awarded a college scholarship.

"Don't think of your missing limb as something that makes you a lesser person," Larry once told an audience of children who had lost limbs. "Think of it as something that can make you stronger. I would love to be the first pro golfer with a prosthetic hand. But I also know that if I don't succeed, I won't be a failure. We only fail if we don't try."

In her autobiography, Dolly Parton wrote,

My high school was small. So during our graduation event, each of us got a chance to stand up and announce our plans for the future. "I'm going to junior college," one boy said. "I'm getting married and moving to Maryville," a girl followed. When my turn came, I said, "I'm going to Nashville to become a star!" The entire place erupted in laughter. I was stunned. Somehow, though, that laughter instilled in me an even greater determination to realize my dream.

Another sterling example of passion is Wilma Rudolph. She simply loved to run.

Wilma was born into a very poor family in a shack in the backwoods of Tennessee. She was the 20th of 22 children, prematurely born and frail. Her survival was doubtful. When she was four years old she had double pneumonia and scarlet fever—a deadly combination that left her with a paralyzed and useless left leg. Although Wilma had to wear an iron leg brace, she was fortunate to have a mother who encouraged her.

Wilma's mother told her daughter that despite the brace and injured leg, she could do whatever she wanted to do with her life. She told her that all she needed to do was have faith, persistence, courage and indomitable spirit.

So at nine years old, Wilma removed the leg brace and took the step the doctors told her she'd never take normally. During the next four years, she developed a rhythmic stride and set a goal to become the world's greatest woman runner.

At age 13, Wilma entered a race and came in dead last. She entered every race in high school, and in every race she came in last. Friends begged her to quit. However, one day, she came in next to last. And then, there came a day when Wilma won her first race, and she never looked back.

Years later, at the Olympic Games, Wilma was pitted

against the greatest woman runner of the day, Jutta Heine, from Germany. Jutta Heine had never lost a race. However, Wilma beat her in the 100-meter dash and the 200-meter dash, winning two gold medals.

Finally, it was time for the 400-meter relay. It would be Wilma against Jutta once again. The first two runners on Wilma's team made perfect handoffs with the baton. But when the third runner passed the baton to Wilma, she dropped it, and Wilma watched Jutta take off down the track. It seemed impossible that anyone could catch this fleet and nimble woman. But Wilma did just that, and earned her third Olympic gold medal!

> *"Researchers found that having a positive attitude about those around us is among the most important predictors of life satisfaction and that without such attitudes, we are less than half as likely to feel happy"* *(Glass and Jolly, 1997).*

I Create Positive Self-beliefs with Good Self-talk

"Self-talk," the way we talk to ourselves in our minds, plays a hugely significant role in determining our level of happiness and confidence. Why? Because we usually become what we tell ourselves we are. Indeed, speaking to ourselves positively is the most effective way to create positive self-beliefs.

Since we now understand the power of choice and the power of our minds, we know that our thoughts can be directed. Why would we allow negativity to pull us backwards into undesirable states, or allow the programming of our past to control our present and future? With effort and perseverance, we can re-direct our thoughts and enjoy positive self-beliefs.

To do this, use the same steps (we discussed earlier) that direct thoughts in positive ways. Just as soon as negative thoughts enter your mind:

1. Label
2. Replace
3. Focus Forward

Here's how:

1. "This rain stinks! Now I can't play golf!
   Label/Replace/Forward Focus
   Gee, that was a negative attitude. We really need the rain and I can play golf tomorrow.

2. "My boss just doesn't get it! I bet he got promoted because he's such a brown-noser!"
   Label/Replace/Forward Focus
   Wow, I was being overly critical there, and I usually don't criticize. I'm going to do a great job at next week's presentation and blow his socks off!

3. "My mother-in-law hates me. No matter what I do it's not good enough."
   Label/Replace/Forward Focus
   Woops—negative attitude. Hey, that woman raised an awesome daughter.

4. "What happened to my life!? These kids are sucking it away and they don't even care!"
   Label/Replace/Forward Focus

Hey... What happened to my positive outlook? They're just kids! You know, I should go outside with them to play and get some fresh air.

5. My wife is such a lousy cook!
    Label/Replace/Forward Focus
    That wasn't kind. I know she does her best. Maybe I should give it a try!

Another way we can direct thoughts in positive ways is to practice ignoring the negative ones.

We all have thousands of thoughts each day. Some are going to be positive and productive, and others will be worrisome, fearful, covetous, etc. *The question isn't whether or not you're going to have negative thoughts—it's what you choose to do with the ones you have.*

You really only have two choices. You can either worry about them, analyze them, think more and more about them, or you can dismiss them; not take the negative thoughts seriously and let them go. Of course, we want to learn how to do the latter, so think on this: When you have a thought—any thought—realize that's *all* it is...*just* a thought. It truly can't hurt you without your permission.

Think of a negative thought as a match that has just been lit. You can either blow it out immediately and stay healthy, or you can let it burn, hurt and scar you. The choice is yours.

Let's look at two examples:

> Karen, painfully shy, was completely convinced that her introversion and her low self-esteem were her parents' fault. Karen bitterly

explained, "My parents didn't do a very good job, and that's why I'm a social failure."

Karen let the negative thoughts fester and wound her; convincing herself that she should indeed be unhappy. Instead, she should have realized that although her childhood was difficult, *in this present moment, she has a choice* and can direct her thoughts. Another example:

> Darrel and Katie had a quarrel just minutes before Darrel left for work. Darrel "blew out the match" and let the negative thoughts go soon after he left the house. Katie, on the other hand, was still stewing and angry about the issue when Darrel came home at 6:00 o'clock that night.

While Darrel was able to have a productive day, Katie didn't get anything accomplished because she spent hours fuming and fretting, calling family and friends to complain and get advice. What she didn't understand is that an argument that happens in the morning is no longer an actual argument; it's a thought in your mind. And we can do with our thoughts whatever we choose.

As you learn to ignore and dismiss negative thoughts —blowing out the flaming match immediately—your ability to do so will increase, and you'll become a more peaceful and loving person.

In addition to the negative/positive **self-beliefs** you're working on, I'd like to suggest you make an effort to eliminate *all* negative **expressions**, no matter how benign they may seem. Your subconscious mind takes it all in—and *anything negative becomes part of who you are.* So we should get rid of the "little negatives" that clutter our conversations and weaken us:

- "I don't think I can do that."
- "I'm afraid I'll be late."
- "I'll never get through this – there's so much to do."
- "If I didn't have bad luck I wouldn't have any luck at all!"
- Yep – I knew it! Just when things were starting to go well, this had to happen."

Other negative expressions to watch for (and discard) come in the form of questions. One of the best keys to behavior change is to stop asking yourself bad questions and start asking good ones. Let's look at some commonly-asked "Why" questions:

"Why does this always happen to me?"
"Why can't I figure it out?"
"Why can't I ever remember names?"
"Why am I depressed?"
"Why don't they like me?"

What are you focusing on when you're asking those questions? Negativity. If you're feeling miserable it's usually because you're deleting all the reasons you could be feeling good. Far better are these "What" and "Who" questions that help us ignore the negative:

"What could I do to make myself feel happier?"
"What is really great in my life right now?"
"What can I learn from this that will make me a better person?"

"Who can I help today?"

"Who loves me? Who are the people I love most in the world?"

I guarantee that if you ask questions like these you'll focus on the positive and feel better. There are two more important questions to ask yourself at this point (reflecting on these may feel a little uncomfortable but this is important): "If I don't change my negative patterns of thinking and questioning, what will it cost me in the long run?" and "Isn't it about time that I start enjoying the results of developing new, empowering habits of positive self-talk?"

By Improving the Words you Consistently Use You Can Immediately Improve the Quality of Your Thoughts, Your Emotions and Your Life

One of my heroes, Norman Vincent Peale, wrote:

> To overcome your obstacles and live the 'I Don't Believe in Defeat" philosophy, cultivate a positive-idea pattern deeply in your consciousness. What we do with obstacles is directly determined by our mental attitude. Most of our obstacles, as a matter of fact, are mental in character.

> "Ah," you may object, "mine are not mental, mine are real."

> Perhaps so, but your attitude toward them is mental. The only possible way you can have an attitude is by the mental process, and what you think about your obstacles largely determines

what you do about them. Form the mental attitude that you cannot remove an obstacle and you will not remove it, not if you think you can't. But get the idea firmly fixed that the obstacle is not so great as you previously considered it to be. Hold the idea that it is removable, and however faintly you entertain this positive thought, from the very moment you begin to think in this manner, the process is inaugurated which will lead to its ultimate removal.

If you have been long defeated by a difficulty, it is probably because you have told yourself for weeks, months and even for years that there is nothing you can do about it. You have so emphasized your inability to yourself that your mind gradually accepted the conclusion upon which you have insisted, and when your mind is convinced, you are convinced, for as you think so are you.

But, on the contrary, when you develop a new mental slant, emphasizing and reemphasizing a positive attitude, you will convince your own consciousness that you can do something about difficulties. When at last your mind becomes convinced, astonishing results will begin to happen. Of a sudden you discover that you have the power you would never before acknowledge. (*The Power of Positive Thinking, 1952*)

Taking action and applying these empowering
principles requires a certain confidence on our
part . . . confidence in our ability to generate
change in our lives.

Confidence

To build confidence, the practice of suggesting Confidence Concepts to your mind is highly effective. If your
mind is filled with thoughts of insecurity and inadequacy,
it is because such ideas have dominated your thinking over
a long period of time. The solution? A more positive pat-
tern of ideas must be given to the mind, and that's accomplished by repetitive suggestion of confidence ideas. Thought disciplining is required if you are to re-educate the mind and convert it into a positive-power-producing plant.

> *Confidence, in combination with a realistic self-appraisal, produces a 30 percent increase in life satisfaction (Sedlacek, 1999).*

It is possible, even in the midst of
your daily work, to drive Confidence Concepts into consciousness.

The conclusion of a study by Myers and Diener (1995):
"Across all ages and all groups, a solid belief in one's own
abilities increases life satisfaction by about 30%, and makes
us happier both in our home lives and in our work lives."

Confidence Concept Cards

Let me tell you about a previously struggling and now
highly-successful salesman who made this idea work for

him. This man put 3x5-inch cards everywhere he could easily see them: on his bathroom mirror, on his desk at work, in his car (on the visor), and in his planner. On these cards were Confidence Concepts that affirmed his goodness:

"I am a great salesman!"
"I radiate confidence and kindness to everyone."
"I am a patient, loving husband and father."
"I am organized and efficient at work and at home."
"Nothing is impossible, because I am a successful leader in every area of my life."

Do you see how this type of positive input, read regularly and believed sincerely, can have a powerful impact on your level of confidence? The lesson is to look at life through lenses dipped in optimism and to remember that "As a man thinketh in his heart, so is he."

Do not forget that if we constantly think of the forces that seem to be against us, we form them into an unrealistic power, and they become stronger. But if, on the contrary, we mentally visualize and affirm our assets, and contemplate our strengths and abilities, we can rise out of any difficulty.

Know this: your level of confidence depends upon the thoughts that habitually occupy your mind. Think defeat and you are defeated. Think confidently and you will develop such a strong sense of capacity that, regardless of the obstacles that arise, you'll overcome them.

Before we move on, take a moment and ask yourself two questions: "What do I want people to see when they look at me?" and, "Is what people *now* see a reflection of what I want to be?"

Reminder: You're in Control

What do you see in your 'self mirror'? What you think of yourself determines your success boundaries and sets your limits. By improving your self-image, you expand your boundaries and extend your limits.

Where is your 'self picture' and who creates it? It's in your mind, and you do.

Your brain is a marvelous mechanism that works for your success or for your failure. Since you're the operator, the outcome depends on your skills. Are you in control? Do you direct and carefully maneuver your thoughts so you focus on your goals—steering straight toward them as you power along life's highway? Or are you out of control, frequently allowing negative and destructive thoughts to take the wheel? Know, without a doubt, that you can daily drive your thoughts, words, and actions in the direction of high achievement. And *with the right tools and consistent effort, you can steer yourself toward previously unimagined joy and success.*

On a day-to-day basis, having confidence in your ability to control your thoughts can make a huge difference in your life. An example of this is Paul, age 68, from Orem, Utah, who suffered a debilitating back injury. He said, "I worked on tolerating high levels of pain and felt *confident* I could overcome anything!"

Give Yourself *Healthy* Self-fulfilling Prophecies!

Self-fulfilling prophecies are statements that help you become what you want to be. They are incredibly powerful in their effectiveness relative to self-esteem. You can either damage your feelings of self-worth or build yourself up, depending on how you use self-fulfilling prophecies. The sooner we begin building ourselves up, the faster we'll progress.

Examples of healthy self-fulfilling prophecies:

- "It's just like me to be on time! I'm usually prompt and ready."
- "I like to meet new people, and I'm good at helping them feel comfortable."
- "Even if she's rude to me I'll still be kind to her, because other people don't determine how I react."
- "I like the way this is turning out. Good thinking!"
- "It's not like me to make mistakes like that. I'll do it better next time."

This principle is illustrated perfectly by the story of a young boy and his father. The father promised his son that if he would practice during the day, he'd play baseball with him after work. When Dad arrived home he accompanied the boy to the backyard.

"Show me what you can do," the father said. The little boy shuffled his feet, threw the ball up in the air, took a swing, and missed. "Strike one," said the dad.

> *Nine in ten people who believe they will one day realize their career goals have strong feelings of competence and assertiveness (Velting, 1999).*

The son repositioned his feet, threw the ball up again, took a second swing, and missed again. His father commented, "Strike two."

More determined than ever, the boy dug in deeper,

threw the ball higher and took a third mighty swing. He missed again, spun completely around, and fell on the ground. His father said, "Strike three, you're out. Well, what do you think about that?"

The youngster stood up, brushed himself off and cheerfully responded, "Man, am I a good pitcher!"

And that's the way we want to think about ourselves!

"The happiness of your life depends on
the quality of your thoughts."
Marcus Aurelius Antoninus

GLASBERGEN

"I'm learning how to relax, doctor—
but I want to relax *better* and *faster!*
I want to be on the cutting edge of relaxation!"

4

I SET HIGH ACHIEVABLE GOALS

"It must be born in mind that the tragedy of life doesn't lie in not reaching your goal. The tragedy lies in having no goal to reach. It isn't a calamity to die with dreams unfulfilled, but it is a calamity to not dream. It is not a disgrace not to reach the stars, but it is a disgrace to have no stars to reach for. Not failure, but low aim is the problem."

Helmut Schmidt

"Nothing happens unless first a dream."

Carl Sandburg

Our challenge? To turn an invisible dream into a measurable reality.

Imagine a pilot coming over the intercom and announcing: "I have some good news and some bad news.

The bad news is we've lost one engine and our direction finder. The good news is we have a tail wind and wherever we're going, we're getting there at a rate of 600 miles an hour!" I don't know about you, but I'd find that news rather disconcerting! Yet people often "fly along" in their lives like that—directionless, lacking energy, but being pushed swiftly along by the winds of circumstances. David Mahoney advises us to heed tendencies that cause us to lose sight of our goals: "The important thing is not where you were or where you are, but where you want to get."

> *Even though they may not want to, people tend to take their jobs home with them at the end of the day. Low levels of career interest are associated with low enjoyment of life overall and even greater dissatisfaction with family life (O'Brien, Martinex-Pons, and Kopala, 1999).*

My friend, Glenn Van Ekeren, tells about his teenage years when he was hired by a local farmer to do the fall plowing. His first day on the tractor was disastrous. He explained, "As I watched the plow turn the soil behind me, little did I realize that by the time I reached the end of the field, the row was incredibly crooked. Toward the end of the day, the farmer arrived to survey my work. The crooked rows prompted him to give me this advice: 'You can't plow a straight row if you keep looking behind you. You must keep your eyes focused on your goal straight ahead.' And so it is with life. Plowing our way into the future is powered by meaningful and specific goals. Focusing on the past, what lies behind, will prevent us from focusing our energies on what lies ahead."

Don't allow distractions or backward glances to side-track your thinking. As you work toward your goals, be like a laser beam focused powerfully and directly on your target.

Oliver Wendell Holmes

I love the story about the time Justice Oliver Wendell Holmes misplaced his ticket while traveling on a train. Watching him fumble through his belongings and pockets in growing frustration, the conductor tried to ease his mind. "Don't worry about it, Mr. Holmes. I'm sure you have your ticket somewhere. If you don't find it during the trip, just mail it in to the railroad when you reach your destination." Appreciative of the conductor's empathy, yet dismayed by his predicament, he looked the conductor in the eye and responded: "Young man, my problem is not finding my ticket. It's to find out where in the world I'm going!"

Where in the world *are* we going? And how are we going to get there?

I Identify What Hurts Most and What I Want Most

At first glance, identifying "what hurts most" may seem a little harsh. But think about it: the characteristics that bother you the most about yourself (for example, being overweight, being impatient with your children, being disorganized/inefficient at work) *can* become your goals, your "target areas" to improve. For example, your thought, *My disorganization really slows me down at work* can become the goal, "I will be more organized. I will do this by cleaning out my desk, staying on schedule, filing items immediately upon receiving them, and purchasing a day-planner. I will clean out my desk by Wednesday at noon and I will purchase a planner today on my lunch break."

Yes, identifying what bothers us most may be the very first step to goal achievement because it helps us recognize exactly what we want most. And we set goals based on stopping pain and creating pleasure in our lives. Since people have created goals for thousands of years, we can benefit from a fail-safe formula that works:

You might imagine that a promotion on the job automatically raises confidence and self-worth. Instead, studies find nearly half of recently promoted managers in the technology industry express uncertainty and doubt about themselves and their new position. Psychologists find that the promotion can undermine their self-confidence because instead of being the best among a group lower-level workers, they now find themselves surrounded by more accomplished people to measure themselves against (Cassirer, 2000)

I apply the 7 Steps to Success

1. Choose only those goals you deeply care about and are absolutely committed to achieving.

2. Write your goals in detailed specifics.

3. Give yourself a time limit.

4. Break goals into small, doable steps.

5. Consistently and enthusiastically take action.

6. Notice what's working (or not) and reward yourself along the way.

7. Continue to make course corrections until you achieve your goals.

1. Choose Only Those Goals You Deeply Care About and Are Absolutely Committed to Achieving

The more deeply you are convinced of the absolute necessity of reaching your goals, the more tenacity you'll exert as you work toward them.

James Allen wrote: "One who *cherishes* a beautiful vision, a lofty ideal, will one day realize it." Belva, age 68, from Vancouver, Washington, understood this. After training herself to become an accomplished musician, she offered this advice: "You must love the thing you want to accomplish!"

How are you going to decide on your goals? Here are some suggestions for "preparing the soil" properly:

- Go somewhere alone.

- Think deeply and slowly about the most important things in your life.

- Carefully consider where you want to be in ten years, your "ideal life."
  Ask yourself, "What do I want to be doing in ten years? Who do I want to be with? What do I want to look like? What do I want my life to look like?

- Then, think about your "ideal life" in five years . . . in one year . . . in six months . . . in one month.

- Create detailed, visual pictures in your mind of your ideal self and your ideal life.

People who are prone to use stereotypes in assessing themselves and others are 39 percent more likely to believe that opportunities are limited for others and themselves (Frome, 1999).

- Use my "I DR" 3-Step Formula:
   Identify your goals
   Decide which are your highest priority
   Resolve to focus like a laser beam

The human being is goal-seeking by design. Dr. Maxwell Maltz, best-selling author of Psycho-Cybernetics, compared the mind to the homing system in a torpedo or an automatic pilot:

> Once you set your target, this self-adjusting system constantly monitors feedback signals from the target area. Using the feedback data to adjust the course setting in its own navigational guidance computer, it makes the corrections necessary to stay on target. Programmed incompletely or nonspecifically, or aimed at a target too far out of range, the homing torpedo will wander erratically around until its propulsion system fails or it self-destructs. (Psycho-Cybernetics, Prentice-Hall, 1960)

The congruence of people's goals with their resources strongly correlates with happiness. In other words, the more realistic and attainable people's goals are, the more likely they are to feel good about themselves. People who conclude their goals are out of reach are less than one-tenth as likely to consider themselves satisfied with life (Diener and Fujita, 1995).

The individual human being behaves in very much the same manner. Once you set your goal, your mind constantly monitors self-talk and environmental feed-back about the goal or target. Using this negative and positive feedback to adjust your decisions along the way, your mind subconsciously makes adjustments to reach the goal. Programmed with vague, random thoughts or fixed on an unrealistic goal too far out of sight, you'll wander aimlessly around until you give up in frustration, wear yourself out, or self-destruct.

2. Write Goals in Detailed Specifics

Writing goals in detailed specifics is of utmost importance. There was an experiment conducted in 1985, with 100 high school students who all discussed, and then decided on their future goals. Fifty of the students merely talked about their goals, and fifty students wrote their goals in specific terms and gave themselves a time limit. Ten years later the students were questioned. Of the fifty students who did not write their goals, only 15% had achieved them. Of the fifty students who wrote their goals in specific details, 92% had achieved them.

> *People who regularly keep a journal, or some kind of written record pertaining to their aspirations, are 32 percent more likely to feel like they are making progress in their lives (Howatt, 1999)*

Our minds can't effectively deal with undefined statements. However, give your mind a definite, clearly defined, laser-targeted goal and watch the power it will manifest! Create goals that your mind can clearly envision and work toward, written in terms it can understand. For example, a salesperson's goal might be, "I will give my sales presentation to 12 people before noon on Friday."

3. Give Yourself a Time Limit

Not only do you need specifics, you need a time frame for success. A goal without a time limit is no better than a wish. You want dreams with a deadline. The simple act of deciding when you'll achieve a goal is a huge step towards making it a reality.

Since time is so valuable, you may consider setting time limits on activities at home and at work. For example, schedule errands for just one afternoon a week or combine them in a timely way. Decide that all your housework will be completed in 30 minutes each day, then work, with your family, quickly each morning or evening to get it done. I've discovered that I can be more productive with goal achievement, *and* my family is more peaceful, when our home is clean and orderly.

> *People who construct their goals in concrete terms are 50 percent more likely to feel confidence they will attain their goals and 32 percent more likely to feel in control of their lives (Howatt, 1999)*

Schedule blocks of time to accomplish your tasks at work. Follow a daily to-do list, giving each task a time limit. When the time for that project has expired, move on to the next one and either complete the unfinished task before going home or save it for the following day.

Another strategy that works is to inform your friends and loved ones of the blocks of time when you *won't* be available. During the most productive hours of your day, allow no distractions. Let your answering machine take your calls and think of yourself as a laser beam—zeroed in on productivity and goal achievement!

A valuable strategy you'll learn, in Chapter 8, is how to use the power of Positive Crisis. It's an important piece of the "time issue" which will help you create a sense of urgency and propel you forward at warp speed.

4. Break Goals into Small, Doable Steps

No matter how large the task, it is infinitely easier when broken into daily tasks. For example, if you were considering losing 40 pounds, the thought is daunting. However, when you contemplate losing two pounds a week for 10 weeks, it seems more achievable. How about the goal of writing a 250-page book? At first, it might overwhelm you, but if you think about just writing three pages a day, it's not so bad, and it only takes a few months to complete a book that way.

If writing a book is one of your goals, this is how it looks:

Goal	Time limit	How
I will write a book	3 months researching	
(About 250 pages)	4 months writing	
	Begin researching Jan. 5th	Research 2 hrs/day
	Begin writing April 1st	Write 3 pages/day

After writing your goal, an additional task is to convert it into even smaller, more detailed steps for your Daily Action Plan.

A word of caution here: while on your goal achievement journey, be sensitive to your level of energy, your family, work, and personal commitments and your life circumstances. Use this as a measure: choose goals you can realistically work on without damaging your health, relationships and family time. You'll know when you're spending too little or too much time on goal achievement. Finding a balance is a key to peaceful living.

Marianne, age 24, recently graduated magna cum laude from a fine university. At times during her education she was so overwhelmed that she wrote her goals in "baby steps" like this: "I plan to take one class at a time, one chapter at a time, one day at a time, one hour at a time, one problem at a time, one equation at a time."

Brady Burr, age 21, is recovering from muscle cancer. I am impressed with Brady's insightful comments and his wisdom at such a young age. He remarked, "Nobody ever *leaped* to the top of a mountain! All things must be done in steps."

John, age 24, from Vancouver, Washington, passed a difficult Certified Financial Planner course. He commented, "The review guide was about 600 pages and I knew I had to cover the entire book twice. This meant 1,200 pages in 40 days or 30 pages a day. I kept to that schedule and even studied during the breaks on exam day!"

5. Consistently and Enthusiastically Take Action

Once you've chosen your goals and put them into small steps, two magical keys are *consistency and enthusiasm* as you work every day, every week, every month toward your goals. This will happen naturally when you are totally committed to reaching them. Goal achiever extraordinaire, Alexander Graham Bell, explained it this way: "What this power is I cannot say. All I know is that it exists and it becomes available only when a man is in that state of mind in which he knows exactly what he wants and is fully determined not to quit until he finds it."

William E. Holl remarked, "You can do it gradually—day by day and play by play—if you want to do it, if you will to do it, if you work to do it over a sufficiently long period of time."

What about the enthusiasm part?

> **"Nothing good or great can be done in
> the absence of enthusiasm."**
> Tom Peters

> **"Enthusiasm is the electric current that keeps
> the engine of life going at top speed. Enthusiasm
> is the very propeller of progress."**
> B. C. Forbes

> **"Like the chicken and the egg, enthusiasm
> and success seem to go together. We suspect,
> however, that enthusiasm comes first. If you hope
> to succeed at anything in this world, polish up
> your enthusiasm and hang on to it."**
> John Luther

Of course you can reach a goal without enthusiasm, but how enjoyable is the journey? While you're working toward your goals, if you do it with a great attitude and lots of enthusiasm it will be much more fun! Here's an example:

When the alarm goes off and you know that means work-out time, instead of thinking "Oh, man . . . there is *no way* this body can get on that treadmill this morning!" . . . instead, think, "OK—here we go again—another chance to turn this body into a macho machine/raving beauty!" Use your sense of humor and have fun with it . . . your subconscious is paying attention!

Dr. Charles Garfield contributed the following experience about a man who lives life with enthusiasm:

> If you have ever gone through a tollbooth, you know that your relationship to the person in the booth is not the most intimate. It's one of life's frequent non-encounters: you hand over some money; you might get change; you drive off.
>
> Late one morning in 1984, headed for lunch in San Francisco, I drove toward a toll booth. I heard loud music and it sounded like a party. I looked around. There were no other cars with their windows open, so I looked at the tollbooth. Inside, a man was dancing!
>
> "What are you doing?" I asked increduously.
>
> "I'm having a party!" he answered.
>
> "What about the rest of the people?" I noticed no one was dancing in the other tollbooths.
>
> He stopped dancing and said, "Good question. What do those look like to you?" He pointed down the row of tollbooths.
>
> "They look like . . . tollbooths. What do they look like to you?"
>
> "Vertical coffins. At 8:30 every morning, live people get in them and sorta die for eight hours. They act brain-dead as they just go through the motions. Then, at 4:30, like Lazarus rising from the dead, they leave their coffins and go home.

They do that every day."

I was amazed. This guy had developed a philosophy about his job in a tollbooth! Sixteen people dead on the job, and the seventeenth, in precisely the same situation, figures out a way to live. . . and live enthusiastically! I couldn't help asking the next question: "Why is it different for you? You're having such a good time!"

He looked at me. "I knew you were going to ask that. I don't understand why anybody would think my job is boring. I have a corner office, glass on all sides. I can see the Golden Gate Bridge, a big piece of San Francisco, and the Berkeley hills. Half the western world vacations here . . . and I just stroll in every day and practice dancing!"

6. Notice What Works and Reward Yourself Along the Way

Positive reinforcement is the way all animals (including humans) learn best. For decades, this has been verified in numerous experiments. Reinforcement is the fastest method of conditioning a new pattern. Linking pleasure to behaviors you want to repeat speeds up the process of change. We can turn goal-striving into goal-arriving with frequent, motivational rewards.

For example, if your goal is losing weight, then immediately reinforce the slightest progress. The moment you choose to walk by the cookie jar instead of reaching in, say to yourself, "Good job! I feel great at 128!" ("I feel fine at 209,"or whatever is your ideal weight) And when you push away your plate instead of taking a second help-ing, reinforce that progress by saying, "This isn't easy, but I can do it! I'm feeling better already!"

If your goal is to quit smoking, don't wait until you've gone a month without smoking; when you've gone eight hours without a cigarette, reward yourself with an ice cream cone or some other "pat on the back." As you congratu-late yourself, both your conscious and your subconscious mind learn to link pleasure to positive change.

Again, once we make even the slightest bit of progress, we should reinforce it immediately. My younger sister, Carol, is an outstanding aerobics instructor. She would never think of concluding a class by saying, "Well, that was a nice try, but you didn't do the routines very well, so I'll see you all on Wednesday and we'll try it again…and *be on time* Wednesday!" She wouldn't have many people return to her class, would she? Far better would be a com-ment like, "Hey, you did *great* today! You worked hard and gave it your best effort! I sure loved doing the rou-tine with you and I can't wait to seeing you again Wednes-day. Take care now!"

But, you know, sometimes it's easier to encourage *others* than to encourage ourselves, isn't it? We need to give ourselves pep-talks like, "Yeah, I *did* work hard, and I *am* doing great! My routine isn't perfect yet, but it's coming along and I'm proud of myself!" Good self-talk is one way of rewarding yourself. Another way is to buy a little something special when you reach a milestone toward a long-term goal. Or take a mini-vacation, or treat yourself to a long phone conversation with a special friend. Be creative and plan your rewards in advance so you can look forward to them. You'll find yourself going from reward to reward and then—you've reached that long-term goal!

Most institutions and organizations understand the importance of rewards. In our early years at elementary school, our teachers gave us gold stars. As we grew older, we received grades, diplomas, awards and bonuses. Don't wait for the applause of others; give "self-strokes" as you succeed at even the smallest task. This is one way it can work:

- Take each goal and choose three or four milestones that you consider to be the most significant intermediate goals.
- Decide on rewards to give yourself for the intermediate goals.
- Exercise discipline. Don't give yourself rewards until you've honestly reached your milestones.

When you divide your goals into intermediate milestones it's easier to see progress and to create a reward system that facilitates your progress.

6. Continue to Make Course Corrections Until You Achieve

All airplane pilots, CEOs and ship captains understand this: staying on-course as you progress toward your goal requires course corrections. The goal is to move forward; improve; develop. And so you first plot a course (set goals), then start the journey (take action in the direction of your goals). From time to time, however, you may veer a little to the right or to the left as you move along because distractions and obstacles are inevitable. Count on them; don't let them discourage you.

Just make course corrections and get back in the groove. Let's look at an example:

Jaime was determined to lose twenty pounds. She had her plan—both long-term and short-term. She was "on track" with her new work-out routine and improved eating habits, and she lost eight pounds the first five weeks. Jaime was thrilled. Then, a series of events knocked her for a loop. She went out of town for five days to attend her sister's wedding, and it was nearly impossible to workout daily and eat right. When she returned home, Jaime immediately came down with a nasty cold, which she had for nearly a week. She hadn't worked out during that week, and was derailed with her diet, too. When Jaime's health returned, she got on the scale and realized that she'd gained back five of the eight pounds.

> *Comparing middle management employees, researchers have found that those whose careers continue to have momentum are 53 percent more likely to engage in healthy life habits than those whose careers are stalled (Roberts and Friend, 1998).*

Jaime has choices now. She can either grumble and give up, or correct her course and get back on track. Course corrections. If you accept them as part of the long-term plan, you'll have a far better chance for success.

Evaluate As You Go

How can you make course corrections without evaluation as you go?

Sometimes, as we move toward a goal, we discover that

our previous good intentions and best-laid plans simply aren't right for us. Perhaps our information was wrong, our assumptions were a little off, our approach was too time-consuming or inefficient, or our priorities have changed. Course corrections need to be made, the sooner the better. Rather than allow this to discourage you, let each detour or setback provide clues for handling similar tasks differently and for making better choices in the future.

> **"Some men see things as they are and say, 'Why?' I dream of things that never were and say, 'Why not?'"**
> *George Bernard Shaw*

"My left brain and right brain don't agree on anything, so I only think with the small part in the middle."

5

I USE POSITIVE EXPERIENCING TO BECOME MY IDEAL SELF

"We are what and where we are because we have first imagined it."
Donald Curtis

I Imagine Things in Great Detail that Become Like Real Experiences

How did you learn that you're good at some things and not good at others? **You experienced success and failure from your earliest years and you built beliefs about yourself based on these experiences, and on the way people reacted to you.** For example, during your first years at school, if you excelled in art, your work was praised. If you repeatedly bungled math problems, you were reproved. You learned, from experience and other people's reactions, that you were a good artist and a bad mathematician. Consciously and unconsciously, you developed your self-picture from your experiences and the input of others.

If you have a poor self-image in any area of your life because of past negative experiences, there is good news! **You can improve your self-image by creating new, positive experiences to replace the old ones.**

You may ask, "Can beliefs from a past which is riddled with failure and nearly void of successes be changed years later?" Absolutely! Studies show that one is never too young nor too old to *change negative beliefs* and start living a joyous life.

The key is in the way you acquired your *positive* self beliefs in the first place: by positive experiences. Now here's some great news:

Positive Experiences Can Be Simulated; They Can be Created "Artificially" in Our Minds!

You see, the very nature of the human brain and nervous system allows you to literally *create experiences* in your mind. Experimental and clinical psychologists have proven:

- **The nervous system cannot tell the difference between an ACTUAL experience and an experience IMAGINED IN GREAT DETAIL.**

- **Your nervous system reacts obediently to what you think or imagine to be true – whether it's actually true or not. In other words, people always feel, act and behave according to what they *imagine to be true* about themselves and their circumstances.**

We all possess the ability to create images in our minds. When we understand that our feelings and behavior are a result of what we imagine to be true, we can change these feelings and behavior by changing our mental pictures.

Dr. Maxwell Maltz discovered these truths through a number of experiments. Dr. Maltz wrote:

> The human brain and nervous system are engineered to react automatically and appropriately to the problems and challenges in the environment. For example, a man doesn't need to stop and think that self-survival requires that he run if he meets an angry grizzly bear on a trail. He doesn't need to decide to become afraid. The fear response is automatic. First, it makes him want to flee. The fear then triggers bodily mechanisms which 'soup up' his muscles so he can run faster than he has ever run before. His heart beat is quickened. Adrenalin, a powerful muscle stimulant, is poured into the blood-stream. All bodily functions not necessary to running are shut down. The stomach stops working and all available blood is sent to the muscles. Breathing is much faster and the oxygen supply to the muscles is increased manifold.
>
> All of this, of course, is nothing new. Most of us learned it in high school. What we have not been so quick to realize, however, is that the brain and nervous system which reacts automatically to environment is the same brain and nervous system which tells us what the environment *is*. The reactions of the man meeting the

bear are commonly thought of as due to "emotion" rather than to ideas. Yet, it was an idea—
information received from the outside world and
evaluated by the forebrain—which sparked the
so-called "emotional reactions." Thus, it was
basically *idea* or *belief* which was the true caus-
ative agent, rather than emotion—which came
as a result. In short, the man on the trail reacted
to what he thought, or believed or imagined the
environment to be. The 'messages" brought to
us from the environment consist of nerve impulses from the various sense organs. These nerve
impulses are decoded, interpreted and evaluated
in the brain and made known to us in the form
of ideas or mental images. In the final analysis it
is these mental images that we react to. *(Psycho-
Cybernetics)*

**You act, and feel, not according to what things
are *really* like, but according to the *image your
mind holds of what they are like.***

You have certain mental images of yourself, your world,
and the people around you. And you behave as though
these images were truth—reality—rather than the things
they represent.

Let us suppose, for example, that the man on the trail
had not met a real bear, but a movie actor dressed in a
bear costume. If he thought and imagined the actor to be
a bear, his emotional and nervous reactions would have
been exactly the same. Or let us suppose he met a large
shaggy dog, which his fear-ridden imagination mistook
for a bear. Again, he would react automatically to what he

believed to be true concerning himself and his environment.

> **It follows that if our ideas and mental images concerning ourselves are distorted or unrealistic, then our reaction to our environment will likewise be inappropriate.**

Realizing that our actions, feelings, and behavior are the direct result of our own images and beliefs gives us the leverage needed for changing our personality, gaining skill, and living joyfully.

Mental pictures offer us an opportunity to "practice" new traits and attitudes which otherwise we couldn't do. This is possible because, again—your nervous system cannot tell the difference between an actual experience and one that is vividly imagined. If we picture ourselves performing in a certain manner, it is very nearly the same as the actual performance! Perfect mental practice helps to make perfect.

One of the many experiments done years ago (this experiment was reported in *Research Quarterly, 1956*) that validated these statements is briefly described in the following:

Mental Free-throws

In the experiment, there were 3 groups of free-throw-shooting basketball players.

The first group practiced throwing free-throws every day for 20 days—20 minutes a day.

The second group never practiced (they were tested on their free-throw shooting ability, like each group, on the first and last days).

The third group never touched a ball. Instead, they spent 20 minutes each day for 20 days just IMAGINING they were sinking free throws. They imagined it in great detail.

The result? The first group improved 24%. The second group didn't improve at all. The third group—the boys who just imagined the ball going through the hoop—improved 23%!

In the April, 1955, issue of Reader's Digest, an article by Joseph Phillips told about how the great, undefeated chess champion Capablanca lost the championship to a rather obscure player named Alekhine. The chess world was stunned by the upset. Phillips told how Alekhine had trained for the match, "very much like a boxer conditioned himself for a fight. He retired to the country, cut out smoking and drinking and did calisthenics. And for three months, Alekhine played chess *only in his mind,* preparing for the moment when he would meet the champion."

I Practice in My Head

Here's another example: Artur Schnabel was a world famous pianist who took lessons for only seven years. Artur explained that he hated practicing for any length of time at an actual keyboard. When questioned about his limited amount of practicing as compared with other concert pianists, Schnabel simply said, "I practice in my head."

C. G. Kop, of Holland, was a recognized authority on teaching piano. He recommended that all pianists "practice in their heads." A new composition, he maintained, should be first memorized and played in the mind before ever touching fingers to the keyboard.

Alex Morrison, a world-famous golf instructor, actually worked out a system of mental practice. It enables the golfer to improve his score by sitting in an easy chair, and practicing mentally. Morrison said, "The mental side of golf represents 90% of the game. The physical side 8%, and the mechanical side 2%. Morrison told how he taught Lew Lehr to break 90 for the first time, with no actual practice whatsoever. The golf instructor explained, "you simply need to have a clear, detailed mental picture of the correct process. You must 'see in your mind' where you want the ball to go, and have the confidence to know that it is going to do what you want. Then, in your actual golf game, your subconscious mind takes over and directs your muscles correctly. If your grip is wrong, or your stance isn't in the best form, your subconscious will take care of that by directing your muscles to do whatever is necessary to compensate for the error in form."

Every Accomplishment Created First in Imagination

Dr. Maltz explained that successful men and women have, since the beginning of time, used 'mental pictures' and 'rehearsal practice' to achieve success.

- Napoleon, for example, 'practiced' soldiering in his imagination for many years before he ever went onto an actual battlefield.

- General Norman Schwarzkopf, in an interview after the victory in the Persian Gulf War, described how he played out his battle plans in his mind before committing troops to combat.

- Gymnastics champion Mary Lou Retton has described how she rehearsed every routine in her mind, visual-

izing every step, every leap and turn, every hand place-
ment before putting her body through an actual performance.

- Conrad Hilton imagined himself operating a hotel
  long before he ever bought one.
- Henry Kaiser said that each of his business accom-
  plishments was realized in his imagination before it
  appeared in actuality.
- Juliet McComas, concert pianist, said, "If I visualize
  the keyboard, I can practice in an airport or at my
  kitchen table. *It's just as useful as actual practice.*"
- Arnold Schwarzenegger, movie star, and Governor of
  California, maintains, "As long as the mind can envision the fact that you can do something, you can. I
  visualized myself being there already, having achieved
  the goal already."

Form a Picture and "See Yourself" succeed

What does this mean in terms of *believing and becoming*? This creative mechanism within you can help you
become your ideal self, if you will form a picture in your
imagination of the person you want to be and "see yourself" in the new role.

Four ways to use this skill:

1. Take 15 minutes each day and relax your body as much
   as possible in a comfortable place. Close your eyes.
   Create a mental motion picture of yourself as you
   would like to be. Imagine, in great detail, your ideal
   self. Imagine your face radiant and smiling; your body
   at its optimum shape and fitness level; your clothes

well-fitting and nice. Imagine (in great detail) doing something extremely well that you enjoy doing, with the people around you appreciative and admiring.

Regarding one's self-image, Dr. Maxwell Maltz noted:

Your present self-image was built upon your own imagination; pictures of yourself in the past which grew out of interpretations and evaluation which you placed upon experience. Now you are to use the same method to build an *adequate* self-image that you previously used to build an *inadequate* one.

Set aside 30 minutes each day where you can be alone and undisturbed. *(Paula's note: I believe 15 minutes is sufficient)* Relax and make yourself as comfortable as possible. Now close your eyes and exercise your imagination.

Many people find they get better results if they imagine themselves sitting before a large movie screen— and imagine that they are seeing a motion picture of themselves. The important thing is to make these pictures as vivid and as *detailed* as possible. You want your mental pictures to approximate actual experience as much as possible. The way to do this is pay attention to small details, sights, sounds, objects, in your imagined environment.

Details of the imagined environment are all-important in this exercise, because for all practical purposes, you are creating a *practice experience*. And if the imagination is vivid and detailed enough, your imagination practice is equivalent to an actual experience, insofar as your nervous system is concerned.

The next important thing to remember is that during this visualization time you see yourself acting and reacting successfully, ideally. It doesn't matter how you acted yesterday. And you don't need to try to have faith that you'll act in the ideal way tomorrow. Your nervous system will take care of that in time—if you continue to practice. See yourself acting, feeling, "being" as you want to be. Don't say to yourself, *"I am going to act this way tomorrow."* Just say to yourself, *"I am going to imagine myself acting this way now – for 30 (15) minutes – today." (Psycho-Cybernetics)*

"Imagine how you would feel if you were already the sort of personality you want to be."
Dr. Maxwell Maltz

If you have been shy and timid, see yourself moving among people with ease and poise—and *feeling good* because of it. If you have been fearful and anxious in certain situations—see yourself acting calmly and deliberately, acting with confidence and courage—and feeling expansive and confident because you are.

This exercise builds new "memories" or stored data into your mid-brain and nervous system. It builds a new image of self. After practicing it for a time, you'll be surprised to find yourself acting differently, more or less automatically and spontaneously—without trying. This is as it should be! As it is now. You don't need to 'take thought' or 'try' in order to feel ineffective or act inadequately. Your present inadequate feelings and actions are automatic and spontaneous because of the data, real or imagined, you have built into your automatic mechanism. You will find it will work just as automatically with *positive* thoughts and experiences as upon *negative* ones.

2. As you go through your day, when you aren't focusing on something else, take a "mini-vacation in your mind." This is easily done with practice. You simply create in your mind a wonderful place where you're very happy. For some, this is a lovely, richly decorated palace; for others, it is a walk along a warm, clean, sandy beach at sunset with someone they love. For still others, it is a simple, yet beautiful room with a large, comfortable bed . . . and a big window looking out onto a pond and a garden of well-manicured trees and flowers. Wherever you go in your mind, that place needs to be seen in great detail. Touch the palace walls, smell the ocean, feel the soft pillow on the bed. Are you with me here? Can you visualize it? You can go on this mini-vacation whenever life gets stressful or when you just need a mental break.

    Dr. Norman Vincent Peale suggested,

    > Fill your mind with all peaceful experiences possible, then make planned and deliberate excursions to them in memory. You must learn that the easiest way to an easy mind is to create an easy mind. This is done by practice. The mind quickly responds to teaching and discipline. You can make the mind give you back anything you want, but remember the mind can give back only what it was first given. Saturate our thoughts with peaceful experiences, peaceful words and ideas,

and ultimately you will have a storehouse of peace-producing experiences to which you may turn for refreshment and renewal of your spirit. It will be a vast source of power. *(The Power of Positive Thinking)*

3. The third way you can use this marvelous tool of visualization—to become your best self—is to heal yourself from past pain. Everyone who has experienced emotional pain and heartache knows that it is very real and extraordinarily difficult to forget. Although you cannot erase the past, you can help yourself heal with visualization. Here's how: When a painful memory forces itself into your mind, **label** it with "Here it is" and then **replace** it with a thought about how the person *should have acted.* Instead of letting your mind re-play the experience as it was, use your power of visualization to imagine what it should have been like. Then **focus forward** as you extend the image into the future, but in a positive way instead of the way it 'played out' negatively. Here's an example of how you do this: A painful incident from the past comes into your mind and you think to yourself:

> *Here it is. I'm seeing my father hit me . . . but I am now reversing that and visualizing him walking into the room and we talk to each other. We don't get angry, and he doesn't hit me. After we talk, he hugs me and tells me he loves me. Dad, if you knew then what you know now—you wouldn't have hit me. I forgive you, and I'm now thinking about how you love me . . . and about how our relationship is now.* (If the relationship is good, that's easy. If

> not, do this) *I am thinking about how I would like our relationship to be . . . I'm thinking about how much more kind you are now. You know, this helps me with my resolve to be a good parent. I learned some good things from you, but I also learned about things I'll never do to my children. So it wasn't all bad . . . I learned, and now I'll be a better parent because of you.*

4. A fourth way you can use visualization is to imagine yourself in the future, doing something that you are going to do: a presentation at work; meeting with the boss; working toward a goal; achieving a goal; taking a vacation with your family; being patient/kind/forgiving, etc; visiting relatives during the holidays; and on and on. Again, you create mental pictures in your mind—in great detail. You imagine every part of the experience, like this:

   > *I'm going to give this presentation to my department in 24 hours. I've prepared well, and I know the material. I will imagine what it will be like. I'm going to get up tomorrow morning with a positive, upbeat attitude and look forward to the presentation. I'll put on my black suit, my hair will look great and I'll feel really good about my appearance. I can see myself right now...yeah, I look great! After a healthful breakfast of orange juice, two eggs and whole wheat toast, I'll go through the presentation highlights out loud, so it will be on the tip of my tongue. Then I'll take my briefcase and drive to work calmly because I've left plenty of time to get there. As soon as I get to work I'll email the*

department and remind them of the meeting. I'll answer my mail and pick up my presentation hand-outs. On the way to the meeting, I'll get a drink of water, and then confidently open the door of the boardroom. Inside, I see my colleagues looking at me with admiration and respect. I go to the front of the room and lay out my materials. I stand in front of the group confidently—with my shoulders back and smiling—anxious to begin. As I present, I am articulate and witty. I remember to speak slowly enough to be understood, and I patiently answer every question. My co-workers are interested in my information and enjoy the meeting. Afterwards, I thank them for their interest and participation and I graciously accept their compliments."

Do you see how it works? Your success in manifesting the "ideal" outcome is built upon powerful, unwavering laws of the mind; so, *of course* visualization works!

Now, *what if* something unanticipated goes wrong on the day of your presentation—the car doesn't start, or during your presentation you're asked a question you can't answer, or the overhead projector doesn't work, or your co-workers are critical and unappreciative? Although you don't expect those things to happen, you can prepare yourself mentally by thinking like this: "If something unfortunate happens, I'll handle it calmly and stay in control."

Imagine in Great Detail and Visualize Yourself as the Person You Want to Become

It's important to understand that although your visualization necessitates high expectations for yourself, you only have control over your own behavior. Your high expectations for ideal conditions and other people's positive behavior *may* not ever be realized. For example, you might have to deal with traffic that you couldn't anticipate, or rude co-workers who don't appreciate you. Remember, that *your responsibility* lies in how you react to your challenges . . . the way you deal with problems. The tricky part is learning how to think, "I can only control what I do; their behavior is not my problem." And then *let it go;* blow out the match before it burns you. Now, if things go wrong with your presentation, that's another matter. You need to evaluate, learn, and use your mistakes as stepping stones to future success.

> ## "Believe in the self you are now in the process of becoming."
> ### Dr. Leslie Weatherhead

Dr. Leslie D. Weatherhead, author of *Prescription for Anxiety*, has valuable advice relative to visualization. He remarked,

> If we have in our minds a picture of ourselves as fear-haunted and defeated nobodies, we must get rid of that picture at once and hold up our heads. That is a false picture and false must go. God sees us as men and women in whom and through whom He can do a great work. He sees us as already serene, confident, and cheerful. He sees us not as pathetic victims of life, but masters of the art of living; not wanting sympathy, but imparting help to others, and therefore thinking less and less of ourselves, and

full, not of self-concern, but of love and laughter and a desire to serve. Let us look at our 'real selves' which are in the making *the moment we believe in their existence.* We must recognize the possibility of change and believe in the self we are now in the process of becoming. That old sense of unworthiness and failure must go. It is false and we are not to believe in what is false.

And Dr. Harry Emerson Fosdick explained, "Hold a picture of yourself long and steadily enough in your mind's eye and you will be drawn toward it. Picture yourself vividly as defeated and that alone will make victory impossible. Picture yourself vividly as winning and that alone will contribute immeasurably to success."

"Great living starts with a picture, held in your imagination, of what you would like to do or be."
Dr. Harry Fosdick

It took Jack, age 53, many years to complete his Masters Degree. Jack reported that what got him through the tough times was "visualizing what I wanted." He said, "I never lost the vision. If you see it in your mind, you will eventually gravitate toward it." His advice? "Day dream a lot! See yourself enjoying your dream!"

Susan, age 29, used visualization to help her through childbirth. In her words: "I wanted to experience childbirth without medication. I tried to relax and visualize the entire process. I told myself that I was in control of the pain; it was not in control of me. I thought, *'You can handle the pain and make it through.'* And I knew the power of the mind over the body: if I allowed myself to think for one moment that the pain was unbearable, it instantly became so! However, as soon as I returned to thinking I could control it—that the pain was for a purpose—I could endure it; the pain lessened and I was able to make it through the contraction."

Kathy, age 28, was miserable while struggling to overcome an eating disorder. Kathy explained that during her challenging days "I tried to keep in mind all the things I wanted to do in my life such as get married, have a family, excel in a career. I thought about how my behavior would prevent me from reaching my goals. I would also try to remind myself that I was not a quitter and the way I was behaving was in fact the easy way out. My advice is to believe in yourself and know that you can do whatever it is you want to do."

Review these facts and consider how you can use them to become your ideal self:

- Anything you imagine to be true is accepted as true by your subconscious mind.

- An imagined experience is perceived and acted on by your subconscious mind exactly the same as a real experience.

- Your behavior follows what you believe to be true.

For those who desire an answer to the question, "Exactly how does this work?" I'm including a brief explanation of how the left and right sides of the brain function. Bobbe Sommer, of the Maxwell Maltz Foundation, explained it in her book *Psycho-cybernetics*

2000. The following is just a portion of the information learned from neuropsychologist Roger W. Sperry's split-brain experiments that earned him a Nobel prize.

How Does This Work?

Communication between the two halves of the brain (right and left hemispheres) is controlled principally by a bundle of nerve fibers called the corpus callosum. Sperry and his students studied patients in whom this nerve bundle had been surgically cut in an attempt to control epileptic seizures. In these people the two brain hemispheres functioned independently of one another. Sperry found that each half of the brain has its own conscious thought processes and its own memories.

In 97% of us, the left brain controls the ability to produce and understand speech; the right brain enables us to form, store and respond to sensory data, such as when we put on our clothes, find our way to a known location or recognize a face. When a word was flashed to a split-brain subjects' right hemisphere, she was unable to speak the word. The "verbal" left brain had not seen the word; the "visual" right brain knew what it was, but could not speak it. When a subject's right brain was shown a picture of an apple, he could not name the object; but when his left hand (controlled by the right brain) was then given several unseen objects to choose from, he identified the apple.

The left brain is logical, analytical and reasonable.
The right brain is intuitive, impulsive, and passionate.

The left brain comprehends an object by its name; the right brain by the way it looks or feels. When you're doing your taxes you use the left side of your brain. When you are afraid of something, it's the right side at work. It has not been fully established what causes these differences in function, but it seems clear that the abilities of both cerebral hemispheres are necessary for a full human existence.

Generally, we think of the left brain as working with the conscious mind, while the right brain tends to partner with the subconscious mind. That's why simply using "willpower" often becomes "won't power;" because, since the way you behave is intimately bound up with your self-*image*, you're not going to change it by attacking the problem with the part of your brain that deals in *words*. Trying to change your behavior through your left brain (talking about it instead of visualizing it) is frustrating because it doesn't work very well.

For example, Spencer could tell himself logically that there was no reason why he should be afraid of public speaking. His left brain would say, "There isn't anything to be afraid of – the people in the audience are just like you. It will be fine!" But in his right brain, Spencer *saw* himself standing awkwardly in front of the group and blubbering his way through a presentation. All the logic in the world wasn't going to change that image! You see, his right brain simply *couldn't process the logic* it was given because it only deals with how things *look* or *feel*. And so, it follows that:

The key to positive change is to create positive images and experiences with the right side of the brain AND to use positive communication (including good self-talk and helpful affirmations) with the left side of the brain.

I Replay My Wins

Has a story ever changed your life? Occasionally, I hear a story that provides a fresh insight and new perspective. I love it when that happens! Here's a true story:

One summer during the 1950's, a bright Stanford University student labored over a difficult physics problem. Finally, he decided to ask his father for help. This young man's father was not just any ordinary guy—he was a Nobel-prize-winning scientist. As the wise scientist studied his son's problem, he asked, "Isn't this problem similar to one we worked on last week?" His son answered, "Yes, I guess so . . . " Then his father asked, "Well, what have you been thinking about this week . . . I mean, when you were walking along, or in the shower, or driving? Weren't you thinking about this problem?" His son admitted that, no, he didn't think about the problem at all. The brilliant father then asked a question which his son never, ever forgot. He said,

"What do you think about when you don't *have* to think about anything?"

His son admitted that he didn't think about science. And then, with a sad expression on his face, the wise father remarked, "Then you better not be a scientist. You should go into whatever field you think about when you don't have to think about anything."

I would like to ask you that same question. "What do you think about when you don't *have* to think about anything? Where do you allow your thoughts to take you?"

Your answer is a marvelous indicator of your self-image. People who are emotionally healthy focus on positive things like:

- their past achievements
- what they can learn from the challenges in their lives
- their goals
- how they can help others

People who are emotionally unhealthy spend their time thinking negatively. They:

- berate themselves for past failures
- blame others for their problems
- resent people and they plan ways to "get even"
- think about their weaknesses and the reasons they're unhappy

Consider your thoughts carefully. Ralph Waldo Emerson reminds us, **"A man is what he thinks about all day long."**

I'd like to suggest:

When you don't *have* to think about anything, replay your wins!

Replaying your wins is just what it sounds like. During moments when your mind isn't required to produce something significant, think about the times in your life when you did something well – when you accomplished something you're proud of. Think about the good things in your life, the happy moments. Recall, for example, the times when you've won something, like a promotion, a scholarship, a race...even a spelling bee! Think about loved ones and people whose lives you've touched for good. Remember happy moments that make you smile. And think about those things whenever you're tempted to be negative, to blame others, or to insult yourself because of weaknesses or bad decisions in the past.

Imagine your mind as producing an ongoing stage or movie presentation. In the Theater of Your Mind, you can play whatever scenes you choose. What I'm suggesting is that you flick back on your wins every chance you get; especially during those times when you don't *have* to think about anything.

Here are ideas of past 'wins' you can imagine in great detail, and some positive questions you can ask yourself:

- I remember the time when my friends and I... That was such fun!

- I remember that wonderful teacher who really cared about me...

- I remember how Mom used to...and Dad always...

- I sure appreciate how my brother (sister/grandma/ uncle) cares about me. He...

- I learned a lot from that experience. I learned to... And now I'm better at...because of it.

- I love this weather! I can...now, but I can't during the other seasons.

- I sure enjoyed winning that... You know, I was pretty good!
- I love those people. They are so kind and good. I remember when we...
- I sure do enjoy a good book; I learn so much! From that book I learned...
- How can I use this information to be a better person?
- What I can do today to improve myself?
- What I can do to help lighten someone's load today?
- What's great about today?

In William Shakespeare's play "As You Like It" he wrote: "All the world's a stage, and all the men and women merely players... And one man in his time plays many parts."

During your moments on life's stage, shouldn't one of your parts be the optimist . . . the builder-upper . . . the believer . . . the joyful one? Flick back on your wins every chance you get, and, as you are lifted by the positive pictures you create in your mind, you'll be better equipped to lift others.

Before we leave this Power Belief, I'd like to share a wonderful story told by Rachel Naomi Remen, MD. She is the author of the outstanding book, *"My Grandfather's Blessings" (Penguin Putnam, 2000).*

> Years ago, I cared for a desperately sick two-year-old boy with bacterial meningitis. Deeply unconscious, Ricardo lay in a nest of IV lines and monitor cords, his tiny body almost hidden by the technology that supported and documented his struggle to live. His mother, a slight

Filipina woman, sat at the foot of his bed day after day. She even slept there, sitting in her chair and leaning forward across the mattress. Whenever any of us came to examine Ricardo or draw blood from him, we would find her there, often with her eyes closed, one hand under her baby's blanket. She was holding on to his foot.

After he began to recover and the life-support equipment was withdrawn, I asked her about this. She smiled and looked away, a little embarrassed. But she told me that for all those days she had felt that his life depended on her holding on to his foot. Moved, I asked her what had been going on in her mind all that time. Had she been praying for his recovery? No, she told me, while she was holding his foot, she would just close her eyes and dream her dreams for him.

Day after day, she would watch him grow up. She would imagine taking him to his first day of school, see him learning to read and to write and play ball, sit in church at his first communion, watch him graduate from high school, dance at his wedding. She would imagine him as the father of her grandchild. Over and over and over again. She flushed slightly. "Perhaps," she told me, "it made a difference.

Dr. Remen then added, "Sometimes we may strengthen the life in others when we have an image of the future and hold on to it fiercely, much as Ricardo's mother did."

"The most interesting people are the people with the most interesting pictures in their minds."
Earl Nightingale

"It's a special hearing aid. It filters out
criticism and amplifies compliments."

6

I ACT 'AS IF' WHILE I'M BECOMING

"Act as it it were impossible to fail."
Dorothea Brande

This Power Belief affirms the importance of living *as if you already are the person you want to become.* It is impressively effective, and well understood by high achievers, because most successful people—at some point in their careers—realize the importance of acting *as if* they already are competent/successful.

One Friday morning, an eager young student at Stanford University stood before Louis Janin. He was seeking part-time employment from Janin, who informed him, "All I need right now is a stenographer."

"Fine," the young man said eagerly, "I'll take the job!" Then he added, "But I can't come back until Tuesday."

Janin agreed, and the next Tuesday the young man

reported for work as scheduled. Janin asked him, "Why is it you couldn't come back before Tuesday?"

The young man replied, "Because I had to rent a typewriter and learn how to use it."

This zealous new typist was Herbert Hoover, whose 'I-can-get-it-done' attitude eventually led him through the doors of the White House.

I Live the Part While Diligently Pursuing My Goals

Using your imagination to create positive images requires imagining those experiences *as if* they were true. Remember:

- Any belief can be reevaluated and challenged (they might be false ideas that you've acted on for years because you thought they were true).

- New beliefs can replace the old ones.

- When you focus, in great detail, on your new beliefs (your ideal self), your conscious mind directs your subconscious mind to accept these new images.

- Your subconscious mind always agrees with images your conscious mind creates.

- **Then, acting *as if* it were true can *make* it true.**

Here's an example of how this "As If" principle works:

Sharon, a brand new salesperson in her company, was thrilled with the product and the prospect of earning good money. However, she was scared to death of *selling* the product, and she didn't believe she could do it. In fact, explaining the most obvious benefits of the product to her closest friend seemed an impossible feat.

When Sharon heard about the principle of acting *as if*, she agreed to give it a try. This is what
she did in her mind as she prepared to give her
first presentation:

1. Sharon thought, in great detail, about the experience
   relative to her physical appearance. She first imagined
   what she would wear: a good-looking business-casual
   pantsuit. She imagined exactly what her jewelry looked
   like, and how she'd wear her hair. She thought about
   her posture and her facial expressions.

2. Sharon imagined every detail of the presentation. She
   planned how she would diligently prepare. Sharon
   knew that preparation would result in knowledge,
   expertise, and confidence. In her mind's eyes, she saw
   herself on her couch reading the material she'd present.
   She saw herself practicing the presentation in front of
   a mirror, and she imagined the exact way she'd look
   as she presented the information to customers.

3. In her mind, Sharon visualized herself communicat-
   ing positively (with both her body language and ver-
   bally) during the presentation. On the stage of her
   mind, she saw herself smiling and poised, standing
   with the confidence of an expert. She imagined
   understanding the challenges of her customers, and
   felt compassion. This gave her insight regarding the
   best way to sell to them. She imagined herself speaking clearly, kindly, articulately and authoritatively.
   Sharon smiled as she realized that she really *could* do
   this!

4. Sharon then imagined herself explaining the benefits

of the product in a way that customers not only understood, but that motivated them to buy. She saw they were excited about the product and asked questions that Sharon easily answered. Then, she imagined one customer asking a question she couldn't answer. She heard herself calmly reply, "Mr. Smith, I don't know the answer to that question, but I'll find out and get back to you this afternoon." She noticed that she didn't lose her composure, but remained poised and confident.

5. Sharon saw herself closing the deal authoritatively. Her customers bought the product and ordered even more than Sharon had anticipated. She was pleased as she imagined sharing the good news with her family at the dinner table.

> **If you imagine scenes like this, over and over in your mind, your confidence level will increase, your performance will improve, and you will be able to act AS IF you already *are* the person you want to *become*.**

Now let's look at the example of Sharon actually *making* the presentation and let's see how she took it beyond the mental practice to *acting as if* throughout the entire process:

1. As Sharon dressed and got ready on the morning of her presentation she repeated this in her mind: "*I love what I do! I'm a confident, successful salesperson who wants to share the good news about my product with everyone I meet.*"

2. As Sharon drove to the presentation, she continued

to fill her mind with positive thoughts. When negative, doubtful thoughts pushed their way in, she replaced them with positive ones. As Sharon walked in the door of the building where she was to meet her customers, she squared her shoulders, took a deep breath and said to herself, *"I can do this!"*

3. Sharon smiled radiantly as she met her potential customers. She immediately put them at ease and connected with them as she asked questions about where they lived, their families, and their activities of the day.

4. Sharon then moved into her presentation with ease and confidence. Because she was well prepared, she boldly described the characteristics and benefits of her product. She then enthusiastically explained how much she and others enjoyed using it. As Sharon spoke, she was acting *as if* she was the person she'd watched on the stage of her mind so many times. She *was* the person she had imagined herself to be!

5. When Sharon closed the deal, it wasn't as easy as she had imagined. For just a moment her confidence wavered and she stumbled a bit when her customer countered in ways Sharon hadn't anticipated. However, she regained her composure by honestly saying, "I understand how you might want to go that direction, but let's look at it this way . . ." and she maneuvered the conversation around to review the benefits of the product again.

6. Although Sharon didn't sell as much product as she'd imagined in her mind, she did sell a good amount and closed the deal with a discussion of future sales.

7. At the dinner table that night, Sharon described her
    experience in glowing terms. She acknowledged that
    imagining in great detail and acting *as if* were the keys
    to her success.

Before we leave this Power Belief, remember that as
you act *as if* while diligently pursuing your goals, you
should schedule into your morning and evening routine
just 10 or 15 minutes of relaxation. This is the time to
both rehearse in your mind, and emotionally enjoy, the
experience of achieving your most important goals. Imagine with great detail – see, hear, feel – and try to create the
exact sensation you'll feel when you reach your goal.

This exercise, if done twice each day, will make deep
impressions on your subconscious mind and will create
neural pathways between where you are and where you
want to go. It will be especially effective at night because
of the way your subconscious mind internalizes experiences while you sleep. Before long you'll find yourself feeling a sense of absolute certainty that you'll reach your
goals. *This certainty motivates the actions that guarantee
success.*

"The greatest way to live with honor in this world
is to be what we pretend to be."
Socrates (469 BC – 399 BC)

7
BELIEVE IT!

Before we move on to *BECOME IT!* I'd like to review the primary *Believe It!* principles. I have included this section in an effort to insure total clarity on the key concepts.

The beliefs in your mind bring about the results in your life. Just as soon as you stop accepting false beliefs, harmful opinions, and debilitating fears, and begin filling your mind with thoughts of goodness and peace, you'll be delighted to discover wonderful things occurring in your life. You will be able to hurdle barriers that you previously thought insurmountable, and begin excelling like never before.

As children, we were powerless when given suggestions by people who were important to us. We often accepted into our subconscious minds negative remarks that affected us throughout our lives. This helps us realize how incredibly important it is to speak positively and lovingly to children—showering praise and appreciation every chance we get.

As Adults We Can Make Choices

As adults we can use constructive self-suggestions and other healthy tools as reconditioning therapy to *change* the beliefs we accepted in the past. New, constructive self-suggestions release you from the negative conditioning that may have damaged your self esteem and inhibited your progress.

Once you understand the laws of the mind, you recognize your power to completely reject all negative suggestions from others. You can refuse to give attention to unkind remarks that, prior to your new understanding, would've hurt your heart and caused you pain. Why would they have caused pain? Because you would have allowed the pain, as you replayed the comments over and over in your mind. You would've thought about *why* the person said it, and you'd give the remark importance in your mind, thinking about it again and again. You may have even allowed those thoughts to anger you. These are choices *you* make. A better way? Blow out the match quickly (ignore the unkind remark) and refuse to allow the flame to hurt you. Go about the business of living with the secure knowledge that you are the master of your thoughts.

Unkind remarks can be like rubber balls thrown at an armored truck. You are the armored truck, totally in control of your thoughts. Simply think this: "I'm sorry he's choosing to talk like that, but I'm choosing to blow out the match. He can't hurt me unless I allow him, and I simply won't allow it." Or, "This is his problem, not mine. I know I'm doing the right thing, and I'm OK."

The following story reminds us of the importance of refusing to allow others to hurt us.

An aging Hindu master grew tired of his apprentice complaining, and so, one morning, sent him for some salt. When the apprentice returned, the master instructed the unhappy young man to put a handful of salt in a glass of water and then to drink it.

"How does it taste?" the master asked.

"Bitter," spit the apprentice.

The master chuckled and then asked the young man to take the same size handful of salt and put it in the lake. The two walked in silence to the nearby lake, and once the apprentice swirled his handful of salt in the water, the old man said, "Now drink from the lake."

As the water dripped down the young man's chin, the master asked, "How does it taste?"

"Fresh," remarked the apprentice.

"Do you taste the salt?" asked the master.

"No," replied the young man.

At this, the master sat beside this serious young man, who so reminded him of himself, and took his hands, offering, "The pain of life is pure salt; no more, no less. The amount of pain in life remains the same, exactly the same. But the amount of bitterness we taste depends on the container we put the pain in. So when you are in pain, the only thing you can do is to enlarge your sense of things. Stop being a glass. Become a lake."

You Can Give Unkind Remarks Power

Whatever power unkind remarks have over you, *you give to them*. You give mental consent and allow unkind remarks into your soul when you replay them over and over. And your subconscious mind will convert those negative thoughts into negative life experiences. When that happens, the person who spoke unkindly 'won,' didn't he, because you allowed him to affect you negatively.

Your greatest power is your capacity to choose. So while you're choosing, choose wisely. Choose to reject negative thoughts, and constantly affirm the good. Pay attention to the good that is all around you. Choose love, life, and laughter rather than lack, limitation, and loneliness.

Many of the beliefs you hold weren't accepted deliberately. Think about it: daily papers and television stations worldwide spread stories of doom and gloom that sow seeds of worry, anxiety and fear. If you accept the fear it becomes part of you and is later evidenced in your conversation and actions. You then convey these fears to others in numerous ways, and the cycle continues.

However, there are those who understand that we don't have to accept the negative thoughts created by tales of woe. We have choices relative to what we allow in our minds. We have within us the power to counteract destructive ideas by feeding our subconscious minds only constructive thoughts and seeking only that which is good and lifts our souls.

Choose to Heal Yourself

Can you choose to heal yourself emotionally, and sometimes even physically, by using your mind? Consider this: destructive thoughts produce negative emotions that must find an outlet. These emotions are often expressed as ulcers, tension, heart trouble, etc. What we choose to do with our destructive thoughts determines our emotional, and sometimes physical, health. We now know what to do with those thoughts and how to convert them from negative to positive. I would like to add a personal belief: as we keep our hand in God's hand, keeping His commandments and partnering with Him every step of the way, our ability to heal, hurdle barriers, and to excel, is infinitely multiplied.

Every part of you reflects, to some extent, your self beliefs: your health; energy level; financial condition; relationships and social status. Usually, the circumstances and level of success in every area of your life are outer manifestations of what lies in your subconscious mind.

How often are you angry? Jealous? Fearful? How often are you cheerful, complimentary, and content? These are indicators of beliefs held in your subconscious mind. You weren't born with negative beliefs and *they can be wiped out*. Learning how to feed your subconscious mind with life-giving thoughts, and learning—then applying—ways to create new, positive belief patterns will bless your life and the lives of everyone around you.

"....and according to your belief it is done unto you."
(Matt. 9:29)

"If thou canst believe, all things are possible
to him that believeth."
(Mark 9:23)

Visualize Your Success

Any picture you conceive in your mind is real to the subconscious mind. That 'real' thought will one day appear in the real world if you imagine it often enough.

Think about the power and common nature of this

principle. Architects and contractors visualize the building they create. . . they see it in their minds just exactly as it will look when completed. The building process always begins in someone's imagination. Likewise, any goal you wish to achieve begins with visualization; imagining it in great detail. The subconscious mind will bring to pass any picture vividly held in the mind long enough. Visualize the end result you wish and the state of happiness it produces.

You will sometimes find that your intellect tries to get in the way, trying to reason and even argue with you. Resist this by setting aside your problem-solving techniques and instead, in a relaxed state and with conviction, picture yourself without the problem, having reached your goal already. Imagine happiness and relief. Remember that the subconscious mind is the architect and builder of the body. It controls all your vital functions, and it will help you become your ideal self.

Build a Beautiful Mental Home

Each time my family built a new home we carefully chose the blueprint and made sure the builders followed every detail of our plan. We thoroughly analyzed every choice and carefully selected only the best materials. Realizing that our future comfort depended on the quality of our home, we thoughtfully deliberated and each step of the process was discussed. Now, a relevant question is: "Do we spend such time working on our mental homes—on our very personal blueprints for living?"

The quality of each life experience is determined by the building blocks we use in the construction of our mental homes. If our blueprints are made with mental blocks of fear, worry and limitation; if our blueprints include verbal doubts and negativity . . . what can we expect the quality of our lives to be? Can we reap luscious fruit if we plant thorns?

We are all building our mental homes each hour of the day with our thoughts and imagery. We can enjoy radiant health, loving relationships and boundless joy if we allow quality thoughts on the stage in our minds. The mental homes we build—our magnificent mansions (upon the construction of which we're always engaged) are our personalities and life stories.

Perhaps the most important life exercise we can "practice" is to create a blueprint of beauty and build an exquisite mental home from that blueprint . . . by filling our minds with positive thoughts that constantly bless our lives and the lives of others.

Overcome Any Weakness

True and lasting happiness will begin to enter your life the very day you have a clear understanding that you can release yourself from all negativity, overcome any weakness, solve nearly every one of your problems, and succeed beyond your fondest dreams. You are a storehouse of infinite intelligence, boundless love, and limitless potential that only you have the power to develop and use, or ignore and abuse. Believe in yourself and in your dream! Choose to become your ideal self, and work diligently to reach your goals.

> **"Believe in yourself, trust in God, then let go and enjoy the adventure!"**
> *Rose Kennedy*

"Our company has a serious energy crisis!
We've got plenty of gas, oil, and electricity,
but we're dangerously low on enthusiasm."

8

POSITIVE CRISIS

"Relief is Just a Crisis Away"
**Relief = Really Extraordinary Living
in Everyone's Future**

What is a crisis? "A turning point in the course of anything; a decisive or crucial time." You may be thinking, *"Another crisis is the last thing I need!"* But stay with me, because this strategy is incredibly powerful in it's ability to catapult you toward goal achievement and life excellence.

I'll begin by laying the foundation for this principle. First, let's talk about two kinds of stress. There is **Debilitating Stress,** a feeling of being overwhelmed and out of control. This should be avoided, of course. An example of debilitating stress: a mother, driving her four children to a birthday party, was hit from the rear by a drunk driver.

Thankfully, no one was killed, but two children sustained injuries, and were hospitalized. The car was completely totaled. On the very same day her spouse lost his job. Debilitating stress, with its accompanying traumatic emotions, will undoubtedly result. (That scenario is, of course, on the far end of the continuum).

The second type of stress is called **Enabling Stress,** and it's a normal part of life. One example: a gentleman, wanting to provide well for his family and learn more about his profession, decides to take a certification class at night. Although he is stretched mentally and physically, he improves his skills and later receives a company promotion as a direct result of his newly-acquired knowledge. Enabling stress is present when we're motivated to study hard in school (to get good grades) and to excel at work (to get promoted). **This type of stress helps us develop our talents and contribute to the world in meaningful ways.**

There's a caveat here: *if we allow it,* enabling stress can become debilitating stress. Now, on to our discussion of positive crisis.

Positive Crisis is a part of healthy, enabling stress. It is defined as a compelling situation where time is critical and action is crucial. Positive Crisis propels you to action with an intense sense of urgency. It is a powerful technique that insures breakthrough achievement of your goals.

Intentionally introducing crisis into your life is positive and good when it gets you over the hurdles of inertia, doubt or laziness and serves as a catalyst for goal achievement!

The Positive Crisis "I ACT!" Success Formula

I ACT!

Identify the Unacceptable Behavior (behavior that is no longer acceptable to you; must change)
Action that Guarantees Success (an action with only one acceptable result: success)
Create a Compelling Consequence (consequence that makes failure abhorrent)
Time Frame (your action has a time limitation)

Identify
Action
Consequence
Time

Examples **applying the Positive Crisis I ACT! Success Formula:**

* **Business person who procrastinates**
  Identify unacceptable behavior: procrastination
  Action: called three clients to meet with him
  Consequence: told boss that he could join the meeting
  Time: scheduled the meeting at 10am on Friday morning

* **Disorganized woman**
  Identify unacceptable behavior: disorganization
  Action: called and invited a friend to visit
  Consequence: told friend she'd see "the cleanest house in the city!"
  Time: invited the friend to come in two weeks

- **Soldier in the Air Force fearful of skydiving**
  Identify unacceptable behavior: fear of jumping out of airplanes
  Action: joined a skydiving club (not required by the military)
  Consequence: he paid good money to join; he jumped on his own time
  Time: a club requirement was two dives a week for three months

- **Singer with stage fright**
  Identify unacceptable behavior: stage fright
  Action: scheduled herself to sing the national anthem for 1,000 people
  Consequence: invited family, friends and music agent to attend
  Time: she had three weeks to prepare

- **Woman afraid to host a social gathering**
  Identify unacceptable behavior: fear of failure
  Action: invited 40 guests to her home
  Consequence: she mailed the invitations and told her friends
  Time: she invited guests to a Christmas party and dated the invitations

- **Overweight man**
  Identify unacceptable behavior: being overweight
  Action: created an exercise and diet routine that included others
  Consequence: he gave his best friend $500. If he lost the weight he'd get his money back, and if he didn't, his friend could keep it.
  Time: he committed to lose 60 pounds in 10 months

Melinda, age 23, from New York, explained her positive crisis 'secret' to significant weight loss: "Put yourself in a situation that forces you to change your habits, where you have to learn to work your life differently."

Jacob, age 24, from North Carolina, shared how he intentionally created a positive crisis in his life:

> When I was younger I was extremely shy. I didn't interact much with anyone. I didn't take kindly to new people or new situations. Most of the time my parents would have to speak for me —I couldn't even order for myself at restaurants. I created a way to ease and release my shy tendencies. I joined a choir and learned to play the guitar so I would have to perform in front of many people. I learned that I could share so much of myself and my talents to help and bless others. My advice is to know that you are special and what you have is worth sharing, so find an outlet, something that you enjoy, and share it.

Perhaps you could take a moment now—mark your place and close the book for a moment, while you contemplate creating a positive crisis in your life. Do you have a behavior you'd like to change? What personal mannerism or conduct is no longer acceptable to you? After you've chosen one: develop an action plan; decide on a consequence; determine a time frame. Try it—you'll be pleased to discover that sometimes relief is just a crisis away!

"There are risks and costs to a program of action. But they are far less than the long range risks and costs of comfortable inaction."
John F. Kennedy

"I'm forming a support group for women who feel overwhelmed by cooking, children, and housework. We meet every weeknight from 5:00 to 10:00 PM."

9

PARTNERING

No Man is an Island

No man is an island, no man stands alone
Each man's joy is joy to me, each man's grief is my own
We need one another, so I will defend
Each man as my brother, each man as my friend

John Donne

Yes, we *do* need one another! Especially when we're trying to change our lives and reach our goals. It's simply easier with a little help from our friends.

I once heard that your friends and loved ones are like pillars on your porch. Sometimes they hold you up, and sometimes they lean on you, and sometimes it's just nice to know they're standing by.

This Pillar Principle is simple but essential to consistent success. Partnering with someone as you work toward your goals provides the following benefits:

- Encouragement – We all appreciate a cheering section!

- Strength in numbers – Most tasks are easier with two (or more) working together.
- Different, creative ideas – Two heads are usually better than one.
- Accountability – We're more apt to do it when we must account to someone.
- Sense of humor – We lighten up when we're with people who laugh with us.
- Fun – It's usually more enjoyable to share experiences with a friend.

Choose your partner(s) wisely. He/she should:
- Sincerely care about you and your well-being.
- Be secure enough to nudge you when you stray off course.
- Be nonjudgmental enough to neither reject you if you don't succeed nor become jealous when you do.
- Keep your secrets.
- Consistently and enthusiastically encourage you.

The Partnering Plan:
1. Share your goals and every detail of how you intend to achieve them. Discuss your Daily Action Plan with your partner.
2. Ask if he/she will meet with you regularly (I suggest once a week) for a heart-to-heart progress report.
3. Invite your partner to share advice and criticism when he/she thinks you're stagnating or regressing.
4. When you meet with your friend, report on your daily

progress since you last met. Talk about how it's all working for you. Ask for his/her honest suggestions and perspective.

5. If you need encouragement in between "partner progress reports," first try to help yourself with rewards, good self-talk, music, food, whatever works. If you're still discouraged, call your partner.

This is the same basic method that Alcohol Anonymous uses, and any veteran of their program knows the value of a "sponsor." This is someone who partners with you, offers encouragement, and throws you a rope when you need it.

Melissa, age 21, lost 30 pounds in three months. She explained that the most effective strategy was "having someone do everything along with me and encouraging me to press onward. It became easier as time went on. My advice to someone wanting to accomplish a similar goal is to "get a partner who is as dedicated as you, so you can both keep checking up on one another. Also, never give up!"

Tara, age 26, decided to compete in a triathlon, but knew that she needed help training. Tara reported, "I had a work-out buddy who I convinced to train and participate in the triathlon with me. We would have daily work-outs, some together, so

Case study research on business executives reveals that 98 percent see their position as the result of plans and strategy and that more than half credit their use of a successful person as an example to help define that plan (Gordon, 1998).

we could help push each other. My friend helped me learn
to run better, and I taught her how to swim. Though we
didn't stick together during the race, knowing we were
both out there to finish was a big help."

Cindy, age 45, was devastated by addictive behaviors
that resulted in her divorce. She said, "This left me a single
parent with a high school education to provide, love, and
care for five children. After many years of trial and hard-
ship we are still striving together to beat the odds and to
be productive. The most helpful of all, during my challenge, has been the love and support from loved ones and
friends. We need to let others help us when we're trying
to reach constructive goals."

Find a Worthy Mentor and Learn

I love learning about people who have "believed it
and become it!" One such person is Wilford, 74 years
young, who shared his story:

"I had a speech impediment in my youth. I was held
back in elementary school, and repeated sixth grade three
times. I did very poorly in my early schooling, with very
poor social skills as well. The wonder of all this is that I
became a professor in the college of Engineering and Technology at a prestigious university. During my thirty-four
years as a professor, I was awarded the Distinguished
Teacher Award, and Outstanding Teacher of the Year award
three times. Additionally, I was awarded the President's
Special Teaching Award. You may ask what helped me
achieve, and I'll tell you. It was a shop teacher named
Wilber Day. When I finally entered junior high school they
put me in a shop class thinking that perhaps I could suc-

ceed 'in this area.' Mr. Day became my Anne Sullivan. He took me under his wing and mentored me. He gave me hope and helped me understand that I could do anything I wanted if I was willing to work for it."

What an inspiring story! Let's move on now, and think outside the box:

Partners Lift and Motivate

One of the keys to achievement is knowing how to make yourself feel good when you *don't* feel good, or when you don't even *want* to feel good. The great news? Your body can change its state almost immediately. Actually, you've done this before, so you'll recognize how easy it is. For just a moment think back to a time in your life when you heard a song that really motivated you or touched your heart. Maybe it was the theme song from the movie "Rocky" or perhaps it was "God Bless the USA." Imagine how you felt when you were listening. You were probably excited, motivated or inspired. One powerful way to get yourself into a happier state is to listen to or create music that lifts your soul.

Another way to lift your spirits is to go outside and deep-breathe or exercise. Exercise is almost magical in its power to lift, and it doesn't have to be strenuous; a short walk usually does the trick. Being out in nature is usually quite therapeutic. Other ideas are to dance, watch a movie, take a warm bath, attend a concert or theatrical production. These can all be "partners" that help take you from where you are to where you want to be.

My personal belief is that the greatest Partner of all is God. He loves us and wants us to be happy and successful in life. He is there to help us hurdle every barrier and to excel like we've never dreamed of excelling before. Those who seek Him, and walk life's path with their hand in His, will be blessed beyond measure. They will come to know the truthfulness of the saying, "Two can do anything if one of them is God." Suggestions of how to partner with God are included in the "Spiritual Goals" section of my *Believe It! BECOME IT! Goals for Extraordinary Living* book—it's the companion volume for this book. (Information about obtaining it is on page 193).

Partner with Time

One of your greatest allies is time. It's true! Have you noticed that sometimes, even though the nature of a problem remains the same, your perspective and your level of intensity towards it changes with time? That explains the popular saying "time heals all wounds." Time can be your friend and partner as you try to overcome anger, jealousy, revenge, etc. or as you work to honestly forgive.

Have you ever heard someone say, "I need to step away from the problem." Both my own experience and that of countless others indicates that this is a very wise approach. Those who objectively see the importance of distancing themselves from a problem are less likely to lose control as they get "caught up" in the heat of the moment. They realize that people prone to losing their temper and slashing out with angry words always benefit by taking a step back—actually moving all the way out of the room in some cases—and letting time cool them down. Time is also good at giving people perspective.

Let's talk about perspective. Think of a problem that's

challenging you *right now*. Imagine it in your mind—create a mental picture of it. Now, imagine pushing the picture away from yourself. Push it farther and farther away until it is very small and far away. Now look at it with a new perspective; it seems smaller, huh? Now, reverse that process. Take the picture and bring it closer to you. Closer, closer . . . hey, it's bigger and bigger! And now the problem is right in front of your face! This usually intensifies your feelings about it. So push it away again until it disappears altogether. Gone. All the way gone.

If you did that exercise carefully and with real imagination, it was mind-expanding as you realized that you can, indeed, affect how you feel about a problem. As you imagine it right in your face, and then move it farther away and watch it diminish and disappear, can you sense greater ease and comfort? Your perspective is a valuable partner as you strive for change and improvement.

Years ago, I read "Lessons from the Geese." This is perfect for a discussion on partnering, and I think you'll enjoy it.

Lessons from the Geese

Fact 1: As each goose flaps its wings it creates an 'uplift' for the birds that follow. By flying in a 'V' formation, the whole flock adds 71% greater flying range than if each bird flew alone.

Lesson 1: People who share a common direction and sense of community can get where they're going quicker and easier because they are traveling on the 'uplift' of one another.

Fact 2: When a goose falls out of formation, it suddenly feels the drag and resistance of flying alone. It quickly moves back into formation to take advantage of the lifting power of the bird in front of it.

Lesson 2: If we have as much common sense as a goose, we stay in formation with those headed where we want to go. We are willing to accept their help, and give help in return.

Fact 3: When the lead goose tires, it rotates back into the formation and another goose flies to the point position.

Lesson 3: It pays to take turns doing the hard tasks and sharing leadership roles. As with geese, people are interdependent on each others' skills and unique arrangement of gifts, talents, or resources.

Fact 4: Geese flying in formation honk to encourage those up front to keep up their speed.

Lesson 4: We need to make sure our honking is encouraging. In groups where there is healthy encouragement, production is much greater.

Fact 5: When a goose becomes sick, wounded, or is shot, two geese drop out of formation and follow it down. They stay with the goose until it dies or is able to fly again. Then, they join another formation or catch up with the flock.

Lesson 5: If we have as much sense as geese, we will stand by each other in difficult times as well as when we're strong.

"We are not primarily put on this earth to see through one another, but to see one another through."
Peter DeVries

"You're right, I owe my success to luck!
I'm lucky that my alarm clock rings at 5:00 AM so
I can work 12 hours a day. I'm lucky that my car has
a stereo so I can listen to self-improvement tapes
while I commute. I'm lucky that my street is paved
so I can run three times a week. I'm lucky that...."

10

PREPARATION

"In all things, success depends upon previous preparation, and without such preparation there is failure."

Confucius

Famous basketball coach Bobby Knight was interviewed shortly after his Indiana Hoosiers captured the NCAA National Championship title. The interviewer asked him, "Why is it, Bobby, that your basketball teams at Indiana are always so successful? Is it the will to succeed?"

"The will to succeed is important," replied Knight, "but I'll tell you what's more important—it's the will to prepare. It's the will to go out there every day, training and building those muscles and sharpening those skills."

There is no substitute for preparation. Scholar, basketball star, and senator Bill Bradley reminds us that, "When you are not practicing, remember someone somewhere is practicing and when you meet him, he will win."

Penelope, age 18, has a dream to become a world-

> *Research comparing students of similar ability finds that the distinguishing feature between those who maintain a strong worth ethic in their studies and those who give up is a sense of control. Those who express a sense of control receive scores that are a full letter grade higher than those who do not (Mendoza, 1999).*

class ballerina. She reported, "I just kept telling myself that I could become the best if that's what I really wanted. My parents always taught me that you can become whatever you want to be. I told myself I could be just as good as the best girls in my class and better. I'd also think and I even still continue to tell myself, '*You've got what it takes, just keep going!*' Penelope's advice: "Be prepared to work hard and have self discipline. Also, you will only become good or master a step with continual practice. Always think positively because you can become what you tell yourself you are. Never give up."

"I will not give up!"

Marty, age 55, from Corvallis, Oregon, shared his thoughts on how he prepared for the Iron Man competition in Kona, Hawaii:

> Twenty-four years ago my plan was simply to get in the best physical shape possible. I trained for an average of 30 hours a week for nearly a year before I went to Hawaii. I think of this as an accomplishment that took much effort and determination. The last 10 miles or so I felt like

quitting every step. I collapsed on the finish line and had to be treated in a hospital.

In the toughest moments of the race, I counted strokes, strides and breaths. Sometimes the pain is so intense that you just try to run faster than the pain, live outside of your body. When you want to quit, you remember how many hours, days, and *months* you have trained for this day and you say NO WAY, I WILL NOT GIVE UP! The only thing that would have stopped me was a broken bone or heart attack. I had blisters on my blisters but I still finished the race.

During Preparation, Avoid Procrastination

At a seminar I once attended in Phoenix, I was making conversation with a gentleman during the break. I asked, "Are you going to buy the presenter's product?" The man answered, "No way! At the last seminar I attended, about a year ago, I bought an audio cassette tape series that I've never even opened!" I then asked him, "What are the tapes about?" He replied, "procrastination."

To eliminate procrastination from your life:

- Openly discuss with your family, a friend, or partner, the reasons you procrastinate. Sometimes verbalizing our concerns enables us to get past them more easily.

> *Sixty-eight percent of people who consider themselves successful say that there is at least one area of their job in which they are an expert (Austin, 2000).*

- Consider the consequences of *not* doing the tasks. Ask, "What will happen if I don't do this?" Sometimes this spurs us into action.

- FIRST do the things you least enjoy each day. Put them at the top of your "To Do" list.

- As soon as thoughts enter your mind like, "I'll do that later" think this:

Label:	"No, that's procrastinating, and that's not like me."
Replace:	"I'll do that at 2:00pm today." (set a definite time)
Focus Forward:	"I feel great when I don't procrastinate!"

- Visualize yourself doing things in a timely manner.

- Affirm each day: "I feel great when I don't procrastinate!" And, until it becomes a habit, reward yourself each time you take immediate action.

> **"It takes a lot of unspectacular preparation to produce spectacular results."**
> *Roger Staubach*

"We're at that awkward age...too old to
blame our parents for everything and too
young to blame it all on the government!"

11

PERFORMANCE

"When the truly great people discover that they have been deceived by the signposts along the road of life, they just shift gears and keep going."
Nido Qubein

"Never despair, but if you do, WORK ON IN DESPAIR!"
Edmund Burke

PERFORMANCE FORMULA:
Planning + Preparation + Personal Work + Persistence + Prayer = Practically Perfect Performance

Planning

By failing to plan you plan to fail. This reminds me of a story told by Thomas Monson:

> Several days ago, while driving to my home, I approached the freeway entrance. At the

on-ramp I noticed three hitchhikers, each one of whom carried a homemade sign that announced his desired destination. One sign read "Los Angeles," while a second carried the designation "Boise." However, it was the third sign which not only caught my attention but caused me to reflect and ponder its message. The hitchhiker had lettered not Los Angeles, California, nor Boise, Idaho, on the cardboard sign that he held aloft. Rather, his sign consisted of but one word and read simply 'ANYWHERE.'

Here was one who was content to travel in any direction, according to the whim of the driver who stopped to give him a free ride. What an enormous price to pay for such a ride. No plan. No objective. No goal. The road to anywhere is the road to nowhere, and the road to nowhere leads to dreams sacrificed, opportunities squandered, and a life unfulfilled.

Your thoughts become clarified when you write them out, and they are deeply impressed in your mind as you read them over and over again.

We've already discussed each point in the **Believe It! BECOME IT! 5 Step Goal Plan.** Although simple, this plan guarantees goal achievement.

5 Step Goal Plan

1   Choose your goals
2   Divide your goals into small steps
3   Schedule your goal steps into a Daily Action Plan
4   Work your plan—*do it!*
5   Review your progress regularly

While we're planning, why not plan to win? William Arthur Ward contributed:

I AM A WINNER

...because I think like a winner, prepare like a winner, and perform like a winner.

...because I set high but attainable goals, work toward those goals with determination and persistence, and never stop until I reach them.

...because I am strong enough to say "No!" to those things that would make me less than my best, and to say "Yes!" to the challenges and opportunities that will make me grow and improve my life.

...because total commitment is my constant companion, and personal integrity is my life-time mentor.

...because I am learning to avoid the tempting shortcuts that can lead to disappointment, and the unhealthy habits that could result in defeat.

> *Feeling there is meaning in your life is eight times more likely to produce satisfaction than is a high income (King and Napa, 1998)*

...because I have a well-earned confidence in myself, a high regard for my (family), teammates, and co-workers, and a healthy respect of those in authority over me.

...because I have learned to accept criticism, not as a threat, but as an opportunity to examine my attitudes and to improve my skills.

...because I persevere in the midst of obstacles and fight on in the face of defeat.

...because I am made in the image and likeness of my Creator, who gave me a burning desire, a measure of tal-

ent, and a strong faith to attempt the difficult and to overcome the seemingly impossible.

...because of my enthusiasm for life, my enjoyment of the
present, and my trust in the future.

One world-famous winner had a plan. Although Bobby
Unser pumped gas in his father's service station in the
1950's, he was determined to become a world-class race
car driver. His daily pursuit of success resulted in winning
multiple accolades in the race car industry including a three
time victory at the Indianapolis 500. Unser went from
meager means to achieving considerable wealth, owning a
ranch, airplane, racing cars, and Bobby Unser Enterprises
that promoted everything from food products to auto tires.

After one of his victories, Unser was asked, "Bobby,
what makes you a winner? Your cars are not that much
better, are they?"

"I found out years ago that winning pays more than
losing," Unser replied. Then he added this profound
thought, "It takes very little more to be successful than to
fail."

Winning is more than quick starts or periodic bursts
of energy. From the point of preparation to the thrill of
victory, winners are intent to win throughout the race.

"When you are in any contest, you should work as if
there were – to the very last minute—a chance to lose it.
This is battle, this is politics, this is anything," advised
President Dwight D. Eisenhower.

The little bit more planning, preparation, personal
work, persistence and prayer—produces winners who are
strong to the finish.

Preparation is the second part of the Performance Formula equation. It is Pillar Principle #4 and was discussed previously.

Personal Work

Thomas A. Edison remarked, "Success is 99% perspiration and 1% inspiration." Nido Qubein observed, "You may have the loftiest goals, the highest ideals, the noblest dreams, but remember this: nothing works unless you do."

James Whitaker, the first American to reach the summit of Mt. Everest, knew about hard work and putting forth tremendous effort to reach a goal. Avalanches, dehydration, hypothermia and the physical and mental fatigue caused by the lack of oxygen at 29,000 feet all stood between him and the top of the world's highest mountain. All of those who dared to climb it before Whitaker had failed. He succeeded.

"You don't really conquer such a mountain," he said. "You conquer yourself. You overcome the sickness and everything else —your pain, aches, fears —to reach the summit."

After all the planning and preparation, if we want to hurdle barriers and excel like never before, we need to just do it.

Ky Won, age 48, set the difficult goal to stop

> *When asked to describe significant regrets in their lives, more than eight out of ten people focused on actions they did not take rather than actions they did. In other words, they focused on things they failed to do rather than things they failed at doing (Ricaurte, 1999).*

smoking. In his words: "In order to stop smoking, I said to myself, *All right, this is the litmus test for my whole life. I can't give in*! When I made up my mind to stop smoking, I immediately began to succeed."

Duane, age 65, had a goal to run everyday. He said, "I go first thing in the morning to help me wake up and get my body systems going. I dictate into a hand-held tape recorder. This helps me feel I'm making good use of the time. I later take the dictation off and put it on the computer. After several weeks or months your body will get accustomed to the exercise and anticipate the lift it gives. My advice: Keep putting one foot forward and then the other."

Madelyn, age 52, from San Francisco, had two great fears. She was extremely afraid of water, and of public speaking. She told this story:

> I was panicked about swimming and about being in front of a group. I was nervous as could be! But I did it! I learned how to swim, and now I am actually not too fearful when I give presentations. The secret is the more I did it, the more I realized that these goals were doable and that I was capable! My confidence has grown through the years as I have done the things I was afraid of.

Persistence

"Nothing in the world can take the place of persistence. Talent will not; nothing is more common than unsuccessful men with talent. Genius will not, unrewarded genius is almost a proverb.

Education will not; the world is full of educated
derelicts. Persistence and determination
alone are omnipotent."
Calvin Coolidge

Washington Roebling, builder of the Brooklyn Bridge, modeled persistence in a remarkable way.

The Brooklyn Bridge, which links Brooklyn to Manhattan Island, is one of the most famous bridges in the world. At the time it was first conceived in 1883, however, bridge-building experts throughout the world told the designer, a creative engineer by the name of John Roebling, that his idea wouldn't work.

Roebling convinced his son Washington, who was also an engineer, that his idea had merit. The two of them developed the concept, resolved the problems others had forecast, and enthusiastically hired a crew to build their bridge. After only a few months of building, a tragic on-site accident took John's life and severely injured Washington, who became unable to talk or walk. Everyone thought the project would have to be abandoned, since the Roeblings were the only ones who knew the dynamics of building the bridge.

Comparing people who tend to give up easily with people who tend to carry on, even through difficult challenges, researchers find that persistent people spend twice as much time thinking...about what they have already accomplished, the fact that the task is doable, and that they are capable of it (Sparrow, 1998)

Washington, however, could still think, and he had a burning desire to see the bridge finished. As he lay in his hospital bed, he had an idea. He would communicate with the engineers by using one finger to tap out in code, on his wife's arm, what he wanted her to tell them.

Washington tapped out his instructions for 13 years until the bridge was completed."

(God's Little Devotional Book for Leaders)

The story of Rudy Ruettiger is another excellent example of persistence. Indeed, his story became the material for the movie 'Rudy', released in 1993. It is the story of a young man with a dream and undaunted persistence to play football for Notre Dame. Rudy's family, friends and teachers told him that he wasn't college material. They explained that he was too short and not good enough to play. Rudy attended Holy Cross, a college nearby, and worked diligently to achieve excellent grades. He applied, and was denied, admission to Notre Dame every semester until his junior year in college. Rudy then joined the Notre Dame football team as a walk-on player. His dream was finally realized during the last game of his senior year when all of his teammates, one by one, turned in their jerseys so the new coach would allow Rudy to play.

> *Those who do not feel they are taking steps toward their goals are five times more likely to give up and three times less likely to feel satisfied with their lives (Elliott, 1999).*

Young Janelle Hanson, age 19, understands persistence. She recounted, "I dedicated over 1800 hours to my dance performance. It was difficult, but worth all the sacrifice. When my muscles ached so badly that I thought it impossible to finish, I would tell myself, *'It's only 2 minutes; you can do anything for 2 minutes! Pull it together and finish!'* Quitting was never an option for me."

Soo Hee, age 45, earned a PhD in a second language. Mr. Hee said, "When I made up my mind to earn a PhD at a quite old age, I put into practice studying right from that moment without delay. And then I devoted myself only to studying."

Howard, age 55, reminisces about the importance of persistence in obtaining an MBA degree. "In my accounting class I found it was difficult to remember hundreds of rules. I made flash cards and used them all day each day. I reread the rules 50-100 times."

Prayer

THE HEALING POWER OF PRAYER

This interesting discovery concerning prayer was reported by Dr. Larry Dorsey in the Reader's Digest Magazine in June, 1995:

> It was during residency training at Parkland Memorial Hospital in Dallas, Texas, when I had my first patient with terminal cancer in both lungs. I advised him on what therapy was available and what little I thought it would do. Rightly enough, he opted for no treatment.
>
> Yet whenever I stopped by his hospital bedside, he was surrounded by visitors from his church, singing and praying. *Good thing,* I

thought, *because soon they'll be singing and praying at his funeral.*

A year later, when I was working elsewhere,
a colleague at Parkland called to ask if I wanted
to see my old patient. *See him?* I couldn't believe he was still alive. I studied his chest X-rays
and was stunned. The man's lungs were completely clear. There was no sign of cancer.

"His therapy has been remarkable," the
radiologist said, looking over my shoulder.
Therapy? I thought. *There wasn't any—unless you
consider prayer.*

I had long ago given up the faith of my childhood. Now, as an adult, I believed only in the
power of modern medicine. Prayer seemed an
arbitrary frill, and so I put the incident out of
my mind.

The years passed, and I became chief of staff
at a large urban hospital. I was aware that many
of my patients used prayer, but I put little trust
in it. Then, in the late '80's, I began to come
across studies, many conducted under stringent
laboratory conditions, which showed that prayer
brings about significant changes in a variety of
physical conditions.

Perhaps the most convincing study, published
in 1988, was by cardiologist Dr. Randolph Byrd.
A computer assigned 393 patients at the coro-
nary-care unit of the San Francisco General
Hospital to one of two groups. Half were prayed
for by prayer groups, and half were not remem-
bered in prayer. No one knew to which group

the patients belonged. The prayer groups were simply given the patients' first names, along with brief descriptions of their medical problems. They were asked to pray each day until the patient was discharged from the hospital, but were given no instructions on how to do it or what to say.

When the study was completed ten months later, the prayed-for patients benefited in several significant areas:

- They were 5 times less likely than the unremembered group to require antibiotics.

- They were 2 times less likely to suffer congestive heart failure.

- They were less likely to suffer cardiac arrest.

If the medical technique being studied had been a new drug or surgical procedure instead of prayer, it would probably have been heralded as a breakthrough. Even hard-boiled skeptics like Dr. William Nolen, who had written a book questioning the validity of faith healing, acknowledged, "If this is a valid study, we doctors ought to be writing on our order sheets, 'Pray three times a day.' If it works, it works."

(*Dr. Larry Dorsey*) I have since given up practicing medicine to devote myself to researching and writing about prayer and how it affects our health. There are studies which suggest that prayer can have a beneficial effect on high blood pressure, wounds, headaches and anxiety. Here are some of the things I've found:

Prayer Can Take Many Forms. In the studies I've seen, results occurred not only when
people prayed for explicit outcomes but also
when they prayed for nothing specific. Some
studies, in fact, showed that a simple "Thy will
be done" was more powerful than specific
results held in the mind. In many experiments a
simple attitude of prayerfulness, an all-pervad-
ing sense of holiness and a feeling of empathy,
caring and compassion, seemed to set the stage
for healing.

Love Increases the Power of Prayer. The
power of love is legendary. It is built into folk-
lore, common sense and everyday experience.
Throughout history, tender, loving care has uni-
formly been recognized as a valuable element in
healing. In fact, a survey of 10,000 men with
heart disease (published in *The Journal of American Medicine*) found close to a 50-percent
reduction in frequency of angina in those who
perceived their wives as supportive and loving.

Prayer Can Be Open-Ended. Most people
who pray are convinced that it can be used in a
purposeful, goal-specific manner. But research
shows that open-ended entreaties seem to work
too. Invocations such as "Thy will be done,"
"Let it be," or "May the best thing happen" do
not involve "using" prayer for specific outcomes,
nor do they involve sending complicated messages.

Perhaps this is what some people mean when
they advocate, "Let go and let God." Many rec-

ognize in their own prayers a spontaneous, uncontrollable quality that brings results.

<u>Prayer Means You Are Not Alone</u>. A patient of mine was dying. The day before his death, I sat at his bedside with his wife and children. He knew he had little time left, and he chose his words carefully, speaking in a hoarse whisper. Although he was not a religious person, he revealed to us that recently he had begun to pray.

"What do you pray *for?*" I asked him.

"It isn't 'for' anything," he said thoughtfully. "It simply reminds me that I am not alone."

Prayer is like that. It is a reminder of our unbounded nature, of the part of us that is infinite in space and time. It is the universe's affirmation that we are not alone.

(Reader's Digest, March, 1996)

Prayer is the last element in the Performance Formula. The sum of the parts equals a practically perfect performance.

Practically Perfect Performance

This is where I address the nitty-gritty of goal achievement. Performance is about taking action. As Nike says, "Just DO IT!" After all the plans and preparations have been made, we just need to do it. We need to exert mind over mattress and get out of bed early enough to enjoy peaceful and productive mornings. We need to be organized enough to spend time working on our goals without sacrificing a full life with our families and friends. To hurdle barriers and excel like never before, we need to have a genuine willingness to do whatever it takes to succeed. Perhaps not only succeed, but *exceed* our expectations!

Six Ways to Exceed Your Expectations

1. Avoid the Perfection Trap

At a seminar I attended in Los Angeles the presenter provided an analogy I'll never forget. He first explained that many people fall short of their goals because they wait for ideal conditions and perfect projects before they move forward. He then said, "These people are like the runner who positions himself at the starting line." And he moved into place as if to run. The presenter then said, "*On your mark*" and he dropped to a runner's stance and squatted. "*Get set.*" The presenter looked eagerly forward and moved into a final pre-race runner's position. Then he froze while repeating, "*Get set. . .Get set. . . Get set. . .* "

His point was well made and well taken. Too many times I have been like that runner, carefully planning and preparing but reticent to take action because I wasn't totally ready or circumstances weren't exactly perfect. Can you relate to this? Suggestions to avoid the perfection trap:

- When thoughts enter your mind like, "I'm not good enough at this yet," Or, "This project just isn't perfect yet," do this:

Label:	"There's the perfectionist in me!"
Replace:	"I expect it to be good, but not perfect."
Focus Forward:	"I'm pleased with excellence without perfection."

- Delay giving in to the urge for perfection. Force yourself to let a little time pass before re-doing or fixing things to make them perfect. During that delay, repeat the label/replace/focus forward process above. Time usually dilutes a sense of urgency and gives you a chance to re-think your tendency to make it perfect.

- Write an affirmation card that says, "I'm a relaxed person who can let unnecessary things go. I practice moderation and toleration."

A study, completed in 1996, at the University of Georgia, concluded: "Those who believe they will fail to achieve their goals are unhappy, but so too are those who believe they will *exactly meet their goals*. Those who are happiest believe they will meet *some of their goals* and will receive satisfaction from multiple aspects of their lives."

2. Reconcile Yourself to Obstacles

On your journey toward goal achievement, realize at the outset that you'll encounter obstacles and challenges on the way. Indeed, distractions, delays, detours and disappointments are part of the process of becoming. Few things worthwhile are achieved without effort and struggle. Hours may be long, complications profound, and frustrations many, but your strength of character is defined by your ability to overcome.

3. Learn from Failure

Each time you encounter a setback, refuse to allow it to affect your self-esteem or your momentum. Instead, ask valuable questions:

- "What can I learn from this?"

- "How will this help me become a better person?"
- "Was this the result of poor efforts, unrealistic expectations or circumstances beyond my control?"
- "Did I cause this problem? How?"
- What can I do to improve?"
- How can I avoid a similar problem in the future?"

You may also consider whether psychological issues contributed. Students of the mind understand that our beliefs and mental powers significantly shape the nature of our experiences. While your projects will vary and your work environment may change, you always take your belief patterns wherever you go. For that reason it is imperative that you analyze, as dispassionately as possible, whatever contributions you may have made to your own failure and to your perceptions of the experience.

There is value in failure. The value lies, in part, in its ability to reveal elements in your personality never seen at other times. After all, anyone can succeed when he's surrounded by loving people, a supportive environment, and interesting projects. It's in the face of obstacles and failure that weaknesses and strengths become obvious. Losing to an adversary may expose weak interpersonal skills and rejected proposals may reveal mediocre job skills. Failure tests our character, resolve, optimism, and our ability to respond in positive ways. Without discounting the disappointment, we really only have two choices regarding our response to failure. We can either allow it to impede our progress, or recognize that within each failure are gifts: something to learn and an opportunity to grow. And within each person is the ability to take failure and use it as a stepping stone to success.

Before setting out to achieve new goals we should ask ourselves questions about past failure. "Why haven't I reached the goals I created in the past? Why have I failed? What's holding me back?"

While you're evaluating past failure, obey two rules:

Rule Number 1:   Don't blame others.

Rule Number 2:   Only analyze past failures to learn from them.

Rule #1 Don't Blame Others

We've discussed the futility and negative consequences of blaming others, and the rewards of using your agency to choose positive paths. Think about taking all the energy previously used for blaming/resenting others/ heaping piles of guilt on yourself, and spending that energy in a positive way—like focusing on achieving a highly-defined goal! Imagine the results! Again, there are prerequisites for this: First, a belief that you can do it. Second, a desire. Third, consistent effort. But oh…the pot at the end of that glorious rainbow is living an extraordinarily happy life!

Additional thoughts on blaming others:

"Nobody is a real loser—until they start blaming somebody else." John Wooden (one of the greatest basketball coaches of all time)

"The longer you dwell on another's weakness, the more you infect your own mind with unhappiness." Hugh Prather

And Glenn Van Ekeren contributed three short stories:

1. A man placed on a strict weight-loss program gave in to temptation one morning and bought doughnuts at

the bakery. When asked why he cheated on his diet, he said it was God's fault for opening up a parking place right in front of the bakery as he drove by. When all else fails, some people even blame God!

2. The coach of a high school baseball team became frustrated with the performance of his first base player. Error after error made it difficult for the other players to have faith in him and winning games depended on his improved performance. One afternoon the coach grabbed a glove and headed for first base to show the player how it should be done. The first ball that was hit toward him took a bad hop and clobbered the coach in the chest. Next came a popper just outside the first baseline. Lost in the bright sun, the ball glanced off his glove and hit him in the forehead. Then a wild throw from the shortstop caused the coach to dive, splitting open the seat of his pants. Exasperated, the coach turned to his first base player, handed him the glove and shouted, 'You've got this position so messed up, even I can't do a thing with it!'

3. A mother brought her two arguing children together and demanded they make immediate amends. The siblings hesitantly apologized to each other, and then the younger commented, "I'm apologizing on the outside, but I'm still angry on the inside!"

True forgiveness roots out negative beliefs. It doesn't bury the hatchet while allowing the handle to remain exposed. Although this is challenging, nonetheless there is a requirement to let go of blame, resentment and negative feelings from the past if you are to move forward unencumbered; free from the backwards-pulling negativity that prevents progress.

Rule #2
Only Analyze Past Failures to Learn From Them

The only reason for looking backwards at your mistakes is to help you become a better person—by learning what did and didn't work. For example, if you were fired from a job, it's healthy to ask why. Perhaps financial troubles caused the company to cut 200 jobs; it had nothing to do with your skills. However, maybe you were fired for a personal reason that you need to evaluate carefully.

When assessing your strengths and weaknesses, one of the best things to do is talk with a trusted friend or relative, someone whose opinion you value. Spend time with that loved one and take an honest look at where you are and where you want to be. Talk about how *you* perceive your strengths and weaknesses, and ask for his honest opinion. Discuss why he thinks you haven't reached previous goals. Then, listen with an open heart, never taking offense. Write down his ideas, and *consider* using them to help you determine your goals.

Another way to learn from past mistakes is to analyze the following areas relative to your weaknesses and strengths. Ask yourself questions to:

A. help you understand what has held you back

B. learn from your past weaknesses

C. prevent past mistakes

D. turn weaknesses into strengths

And then create healthy, forward-focusing statements that will help you progress.

Psychological (thoughts, words and actions)

A Question: "What thoughts/words/actions have kept me from my goal?

Statement: "I think positive thoughts and only do that which takes me toward my goals."

B Question: "What bad habit should I eliminate?"

Statement: "I can stop procrastinating and begin following through right away."

C Question: "What mistakes have I made that I can learn from?"

Statement: "I've used negative self-talk and that's hurt me. Now I think only positive thoughts about myself and others."

D Question: "What weakness can I turn around and make a strength?"

Statement: "I've been too critical of others. Now I look for people's good qualities."

Environment (home, work space, recreational environment)

A Question: "What circumstances do I put myself in that make it difficult to succeed?"

Statement: "I create an environment that helps me reach my goals."

B Question: "What can I learn from my past weaknesses?"

Statement: "I've always had a huge "snack" when I got home from work, and now I eat a piece of fruit and then wait until dinner."

C Question: "What can I do to prevent mistakes?"

Statement: "I put a lock on the refrigerator." (Just kidding) "I have my fruit snack waiting and a note to remind me of my resolve, until it becomes a habit."

D Question: "How can I turn my weakness into a strength?"

Statement: "I use lots of positive reinforcement and partner with caring loved ones who help me reach my goals."

Relationships (romantic, family, business, social)

A Question: "What people in my life weaken me? Who strengthens me?"

Statement: "I surround myself with people who help me reach my goals."

B Question: "I'll list the people who pull me down and who lift me up." (Write their names down)

Statement: "Since I know who weakens me, I don't associate with them. I only associate with people who strengthen me."

C Question: "Can I prevent mistakes by associating only with good, strong people who truly care about my well-being?"

Statement: "I prevent mistakes by associating with people who truly care about my well-being. I avoid all others."

D Question: "How can I turn past relationship failures into strengths?"

Statement: "I know what doesn't work with relationships, and I know what does. I only do those things that contribute to healthy, peaceful relationships."

As you've moved through this book, you've spent some time examining what's held you back, and you've looked at things that have possibly prevented you from achieving past goals. If you took the time to do the exercises above, you've questioned your limiting beliefs and you now have the skills to move forward.

4. Don't Give In to Worry

Sometimes when we encounter setbacks we allow those experiences to prevent us from enthusiastic forward movement because of worry and anxiousness. We allow failure to discourage us and shake our self-beliefs. Have the strength of character to eliminate self-recrimination. Rather, spring back with a healthy rebound after defeat and realize that worry is like a rocking chair: it keeps you busy, but it doesn't get you anywhere!

All outstanding achievers share one trait: they are convinced of the importance of their goals and they pursue them with great tenacity, refusing to allow anything—including failure and concern—to keep them from success. Reserve your precious energy for a laser beam focus on your goals.

5. Schedule Time to Review Progress

Set aside a regular time each day, week, month, and year to review your goal progress. When goal review is a normal part of your schedule it's easier than if you have to "work it in."

Use your "Review Progress" time as a brief routine checkup (your yearly review may take longer), not as an exercise in faultfinding. Daily progress will usually be negligible, but greater progress is obvious when reviewing past weeks, months, and years.

Have an objective and subjective measurement for each goal. An example of an objective measurement:

Daily: "I called three more contacts today than yesterday."

Monthly: "I sold six more products this month than last month."

For subjective measurement, ask yourself, "How do I feel about my progress? How is my attitude? How strongly am I committed to my goals? What is my confidence level?"

Daily: "Today I sell my product (service) more confidently than I did last week."

Monthly: "I'm really proud of the progress I've made!"

6. Goal Affirmation

Power Belief #2, "I Am Joyful and Confident" included information about using Confidence Concept cards to improve your self-beliefs. Those differ from Goal Affirmations because Confidence Concepts talk about self. Goal Affirmations address your positive beliefs concerning your goals. These statements describe the emotions you feel when you reach your goal.

Goal Affirmations are beneficial as they help you create the picture images in your mind that become like real experiences. They also impress the goal over and over on your subconscious mind which virtually guarantees goal achievement.

Twice each day (morning and night) you should read and say your Goal Affirmations with conviction. These statements are written as if you've already achieved your goals. Remember, your subconscious mind can't tell the difference between reality and something imagined in great detail. Your Goal Affirmations serve as visualization tools to help you create a "real experience." Combine that with acting *as if* while you're diligently pursuing your goals, and success will be yours! Here are sample Goal Affirmations for the first twelve goals in the *"Goals For Extraordinary Living"* book. There are three things to remember when writing Goal Affirmations. Always use:

1. Personal pronoun ("I")
2. Present tense verbs ("feel")
3. Emotion words ("pleased")

Work Goals	**Goal Affirmations**
1. To be more appreciated	"I feel great when my boss congratulates me for my excellent work."
2. To be more influential	"It makes me happy when my boss asks my opinion."
3. To be more competent	"I'm pleased when I see the good work I'm doing."
4. To be more creative	"My creative imagination is one of my best talents."
5. To be more efficient	"I feel good when I finish my work quickly and efficiently."
6. To get promoted	"I am thrilled that my boss offered me the new position!"

Physical Goals	Goal Affirmations
1. To be more attractive	"I am delighted when I look in the mirror."
2. To be healthier	"It's great to know that I'm almost never sick."
3. To weigh more or less	"I feel great at 128!" Or, "I feel fine at 209!"
4. To be more physically fit	"I like the way my body looks and feels."
5. To have more energy	"It feels super to have so much energy!"
6. To be stronger	"I'm happy to know I can lift my own body weight."

Successful people have control of their lives, with clearly defined goals and purposes that they affirm. They know where they're going and they don't leave things to chance, but make life happen for themselves and their loved ones. On the other hand, many people seem to have a weekly goal of simply "making it to Friday," so they can celebrate on the weekend.

A goal-seeker's greatest hope is to not only achieve the goal but to exceed it. For example, if your goal is to be more influential at work, you're most happily surprised when the owner invites you to be the new vice president! Those who follow the Believe It! BECOME IT! strategies discover that their fondest dreams become realities. Then, the next step is to set new goals and move up to the next level of living.

DAILY ACTION PLAN

MORNING

1. Immediately upon arising, go to a special place in your home where you can spend at least 5 minutes relaxed and quiet as you imagine achieving your major goals. Imagine, in great detail, accomplishing each goal. Envision your relief and joy as you reach each goal. Project your mind forward to success.

2. As you get ready for the day, read the positive thoughts, power beliefs, and affirmations on the 3x5 cards posted in your bathroom. They're like this:
    *   "I create positive, healthy changes in my life."
    *   "I am joyful and confident."
    *   "I feel great at 128!"
    *   "I am a highly successful salesperson."
    *   "I enjoy meeting people and selling product that I believe in."

3. Make a "To Do" list of things you intend to accomplish that day. Be sure and add the items you didn't accomplish the day before. Write your list in small, doable steps. Set a time limit for each item, if you wish.

DURING THE DAY

1. Do the most important things first and cross off each item as you complete it.

2. Focus on listed tasks only; don't get distracted. Delegate all you can.

3. Throughout the day be positive, grateful, and imagine success.

4. No matter how busy you are, do one thing (even if it's small) for yourself, and one kind thing for someone else.

EVENING

1. Take time at the end of the day to repeat Morning Step 1.

2. As you get ready for bed, repeat Morning Step 2.

3. Right before you go to sleep think thoughts of gratitude and love.

> *Successful people spend at least fifteen minutes every day thinking about what they are doing and can do to improve their lives. (Niven, 1998)*

"Whatever I have tried to do in my life, I have tried with all my heart to do well."
Charles Dickens

12

BECOME IT!

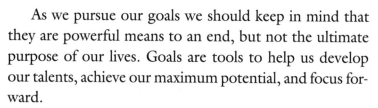

As we pursue our goals we should keep in mind that they are powerful means to an end, but not the ultimate purpose of our lives. Goals are tools to help us develop our talents, achieve our maximum potential, and focus forward.

A study completed in 1996, by Emmons and Kaiser, revealed that working toward goals is critical to "life satisfaction." However, achieving goals by themselves doesn't provide long-term happiness. That's achieved in the process of becoming—as you learn and grow, as you hurdle obstacles and meet challenges—as you discover your inner strength and also your dependence on God. The deepest and most long-lasting sense of joy and fulfillment comes not from achieving goals of material value, but from learning how to love (God, yourself, and others) and contribute in meaningful ways to your fellow man and to the world.

In truth, we are constantly in a state of becoming. Never will there be a time that either you or I can declare, "*Now* I have become!" And that's good news because it means we can continue learning, growing, and progressing as long as we have breath. We can continue setting goals and improving ourselves, no matter how old we are!

I'd like to share highlights from the stories of people who believed it and became it. These are just a few of the many respondents to a survey that asked:

1. Briefly describe your accomplishment.

2. What techniques or specific thoughts helped you through the tough moments?

3. What advice would you give a person wanting to accomplish the same goal?

Janette, age 54:

> In May of 1996, I was viciously attacked and mauled by 2 dogs while the drunken owner of the dogs stood by. I sustained multiple bites and lacerations and was rendered helpless on the ground. Through the courageous help of my 23 year old daughter and divine intervention, I was rescued. This experience caused me to develop a severe case of Post Traumatic Stress Disorder (PTSD) which left me mentally disabled. Previous to this experience I had my own real estate business and was listed among the top 1% of realtors nationwide, based on income. After this experience, I could not even leave my own home. I suffered from severe panic attacks, hallucination and sleep deprivation. I lost my ability to work with numbers and

follow a simple cooking recipe. I totally lost my business and my feelings of self worth. Needless to say, I developed serious depression.

From the beginning, I relied upon my dear family for support. Then, after months turned into years, I felt I was a burden and not a blessing. I pulled away and felt very alone.

The first 2 years after this experience, I spent in counseling and court. The court system left me feeling more personally attacked and vulnerable than the dogs. I received professional counseling and also help from God.

Now, 6 years later, I am at peace. I feel that I am a contributing member of my family and society. No, I am not a professional Realtor. I still have PTSD and cannot confront aggressive dogs. Nor have I chosen to return to full time employment. What I have chosen to "be" is a fantastic wife to my loving husband and a magnificent mother and grandmother to 4 amazing children and 8 grandchildren. I have chosen to "be" cheerful as I fulfill my domestic duties and nurturing opportunities. And, I now gratefully sleep through the night.

My greatest accomplishment is what I am learning along this long journey...those precious truths that I now know. Each lesson has come at great personal cost and effort and I treasure each one. I have learned that it is only through adversity that man comes to know God. To this day, I continue to learn and feel profound gratitude for my adversity.

Jeff, age 49, shares how he and his wife "not only survived but thrived" during her bout with stage three breast cancer. His suggestions:

- *Trust in the Lord.* Cancer is so overwhelming, unpredictable, and uncontrollable that at first we were frightened and despairing. But then we gave the cancer to the Lord and let Him worry about it. We felt ourselves encircled in the arms of His love. We weren't assured of a cure but were assured of His love.

- *Appreciate every day.* With 8-9 months of chemo, surgery, chemo again, and then radiation, my wife had many trials. But we learned to appreciate every day, especially the good days, as a gift and miracle from God.

- *Focus on what you can do, not what you can't do.* During chemo my wife's immune system was so low that she couldn't leave the house. Instead of bemoaning her confinement, my wife was happy that she could now spend time doing photo albums or reading to our five-year-old son. Instead of bemoaning the fact that I was given all of the outside household responsibilities, I rejoiced that I had an excuse to spend so much more time with my children.

- *Keep things in perspective.* After dealing with this big trial, we came to realize that most of the other things in life that were frustrating were little annoyances, not worthy of our negative emotion.

- *Set priorities.* In reality, all of us suffer from a terminal disease...life. Our days in mortality are numbered. Cancer helped us to see that clearly, so we began to make better choices about how we spent our days.

Cheryl, age 24:

I recovered from chronic illness and depression and overcome a drug dependency. What helped me going through the tough moments was that I imagined great stories to parallel and describe the struggles that were going on inside of me. The difficulties I was facing, the internal struggles and pain (physical and emotional), the cravings for the drugs, and the depression and fear that assailed me were the terrible monsters that I, as the hero of the story, had to conquer. And even more important, it was my task to establish and create a richly beautiful world inside myself. How many true heroes happily signed up for their difficult tasks, after all?

I am working toward the creation of something positive instead of merely the eradication of the negative. I have found that my thoughts and beliefs have physical effects on my body. The more I pay attention to this phenomenon, the more I am able to see it. This does not mean that an illness or addiction is "all in your mind." Rather, it means that your body, mind, emotions, etc. are all part of an incredible, intelligent creation-in-process that actually has the capacity to guide its own creation. So many people seem to think that their life doesn't matter much. They would be uncomfortable with the idea that their lives are really epic in proportion. I believe the truth is that we are powerful people, with the capability of creating something beautiful and full of joy. We are all adventures. Life is rich.

Becky Anne, age 19:

I personally overcame an eating disorder. It began with an "innocent" obsession to exercise and a restrictive diet. I had decided to spend my summer training for my upcoming volleyball season. After losing a lot of weight and reaching an athletic peak, I liked my results, but continually craved foods that were "off limits." Losing all internal cues of hunger, I fell into the dangerous cycle of binging and purging.

I tried to think of long-term effects, all the while focusing on the small victories and baby steps. I would remind myself that if I let these problems persist it would severely affect my physical health, my ability to consistently perform mentally and athletically, my ability to have children, etc. I tried not to let setbacks get me down. Each day was a new opportunity to improve and get better. I continually prayed for help, but especially in moments of weakness. I increased my service to others so I could forget about myself. In fact, while recognizing and continually acknowledging the problem, I tried to forget about my food and exercise obsessions completely. I wouldn't let my mind dwell on food, exercise, my figure, or anything associated. I planned out a balanced exercise schedule and stuck with it, and then tried to regain those natural cues of hunger and satiety. Though it took a long time, with many moments of despair and defeat mixed in, I was finally able to trust myself. It felt so good to regain that control and confidence in myself.

I would recommend that a person wanting to accomplish the same goal do the same things I did, such as: take small steps to small victories while focusing on the long-term effects of their decisions; serve others to forget themselves; get in tune with their spiritual side and plea for help; and ultimately focus on finding a natural balance pertaining to exercise and diet. One thing that I did not do until after struggling alone for a long time was to confide in a trusted friend, sibling, parent, etc. I would recommend that those hoping to accomplish the same goal should do this more quickly than I, so as not to feel isolated and alone. Hiding your problem only increases the negative effects as you put up a front and avoid questioning. Having that extra support will strengthen and comfort you, and when you lose confidence in yourself you have one more resource to turn to.

David, age 24:

For quite awhile I hated my step-father. While he was dating my mom he was very nice to me. Once they got married, however, he would lecture me incessantly and ruin any social activity I tried to participate in. There was always something I was doing wrong. It seemed like just about everything he did told me how unimportant I was. One day my parents came home and told me they had bought a house about 80 miles away just because they liked it. They never bothered to ask for any input from me. For the next two years, I commuted about 180 miles a day to high school and back. My stepfather even "helped" me get a demeaning job that was awful. Consequently, I hated him. Just hearing him say anything made me boil inside. Now, however, I get along well with him and even consider him a good friend. There isn't even any awkwardness between us.

To get rid of the anger I had to let go of everything I was so mad at him for. I tried to look for the ways that he would try to show me that he cared. Noticing just a few of these helped me to forgive those things I had deemed unforgivable. My plan of action was to minimize confrontation and try to focus on other things. Once I decided that I wanted things to be better, it was my plan to not let anything bother me, and to always keep a positive attitude about our relationship.

My advice? Let go of the hate. Letting yourself be consumed by hate only makes you unable to do anything else. You have a choice of how to respond. Look for the good in people and learn not to dwell on negative things.

Jamilyn, age 25:

About 5 years ago I was diagnosed with a rare blood disorder. There were no treatments or medication made available to me. I was in the darkest point of my life. I did not know if I was going to live or die. I was young and filled with so much life. I felt as if life had been ripped from my grasp and there was nothing I could do to change it. However, I fought and I am still alive today! I am able to find joy in life. I am viable and living.

There were points of time during my illness that I did not think I could live another day this way. I went from being a fun loving, carefree, free spirit to sleeping almost 18 hours a day, every day, for a couple years. I gained a tremendous amount of weight. Everything that brought joy to my life was suddenly something I was no longer able to participate in. It hit me almost over night. I can distinctly remember the day I started feeling sick. I felt like I had been in a terrible accident and it was the next day. I could not function. I could not even sit up long enough nor did I have the energy to read. My youngest sister would sit on the bed next to me and read to me. I tried to think of things I was grateful for on a regular basis. I must admit there were many days that I could not think of anything that I was grateful for!

What advice would I give? Never give up! You never know why these things happen until way after they are done. Even then you may never know why this needed to come to pass. But through every trial you become a better person if you let yourself become better. You need to focus on others. You need to lose yourself in service and you will find happiness. When you let yourself get so wrapped up in "you," you stand to lose everything. Through hard things great things can come to pass. Never give up looking for a solution to the problem. Do anything in your power to change a situation you are not happy with. I have become more than I was. I have learned compassion and empathy towards people who are suffering. I refocused my goals.

How inspiring are the stories of men and women who hurdle barriers and overcome obstacles on their way to success! What sets them apart from those who live discontented lives, wasting their years in unhappiness?

The difference lies in people's ability to **believe that they can** create positive change in their lives; in their **knowledge of how** to do it, and in their **will to become** their ideal selves.

This is illustrated by the well-known story of the eagle:

One day a naturalist inquired of a farmer why an eagle, the king of all birds, was confined in the barnyard with the chickens.

The farmer replied, "I nursed the injured little bird back to health and have raised it in the barnyard with the chickens. It has never learned to fly. This fine eagle eats chicken food and behaves as chickens behave. I don't think it will ever fly."

"I disagree!" argued the naturalist, "It has the heart of an eagle and can surely be taught to fly!"

After talking it over, the two men agreed to find out whether this was possible. Gently the naturalist took the eagle in his arms and said, "You belong to the sky and not to the earth. Stretch forth your winds and fly!"

The eagle, however, saw the chickens eating and jumped down to join them.

The following day the naturalist took the eagle up on the roof of a house and urged him again, saying, "You are an eagle! Stretch forth your wings and fly!" But the eagle was afraid and hopped down to the familiar chicken coop.

On the third day the naturalist rose early and took the eagle out of the barnyard to the top of a mountain. There he held the majestic bird high in the air and encouraged him again, declaring, "You are an eagle—king of all birds! Stretch forth your wings and fly!"

The eagle looked down at the barnyard below and then up to the sky. Still he did not fly. Then the naturalist lifted him straight toward the sun and the eagle began to tremble. Slowly he spread his magnificent wings. And, stretching his regal neck, the mighty eagle sounded a triumphant cry and lifted off—soaring toward the heavens.

Like the eagle, if you've thought of yourself as something that you *aren't*, you can make the choice to *become what you really are*!

You may have made the mistake of accepting false beliefs and living as if they were true. The *real* truth is, however, you are like the eagle—with the potential to soar—as you hurdle every barrier and excel like never before! Remember, you must *believe* in the person you want to *become*. **Believe it, and you'll become it!**

A MESSAGE FROM PAULA

I've so enjoyed sharing this book with you! Simply stated, *Believe It! BECOME IT!* is a series of principles for living a happy life. They resonate as truth because they are age-old principles that countless people have tried and tested in the laboratory of life, and found them to be undeniably true.

- **Power Beliefs** – Provide personal strength, emotional freedom, boundless joy, and more

- **Positive Crisis** – A valuable technique that catapults you toward goal achievement

- **Partnering** – A common-sense strategy for success

- **Preparation** – A key ingredient for excellence

- **Performance** – A winning combination of action steps

In addition to the principles, I shared examples of people who have believed it and become it. I told their stories to demonstrate that through the same methods you can obtain similar results. But, of course, reading isn't enough. This book is designed not merely to be read but to be *experienced*. While you can acquire information from reading the Power Principles, they can't possibly be agents for change until you put forth the effort to apply them in your life.

I have absolute confidence and unwavering belief in the power of these principles to change lives in positive, dramatic ways. It will give me great happiness to know that you've used the principles and they've blessed your life. I invite you to contact me and share your story; I'd love to hear from you!

With all of my heart I wish you success. I encourage you to pursue your dreams and strive for excellence. *Believe* that you can hurdle all barriers in your life's path. *Believe* that you can dream big dreams and make them come true. *Become* your ideal self and excel like never before. *Become* the person you were created to be, so you can accomplish all that you were put on this earth to do.

May God's richest blessings be yours as you strive to believe it and become it.

Paula

You may contact Paula Fellingham on her website:
www.PaulaFellingham.com

Or call her office: 866.469.6636, or email her:
pfellingham@gmail.com

"Enjoy incredible, positive changes as you apply the Believe It! BECOME IT! principles in your life – today!"

Believe It! BECOME IT! Success Program

---

1. **Believe It! BECOME IT!**
   Goals for Extraordinary Living

   This valuable 250 page book is the companion volume to Believe It! BECOME IT! and provides 72 life-changing goals. For each goal, there are suggestions of *how* to achieve it. Additionally, there's a *positive crisis* idea for each goal—to guarantee success! The book includes 6 goals for each of the 12 months of the year. You may choose exclusively from the 72 goals offered, or they can supplement your own personal goals. This revolutionary program saves goal-setters valuable time and effort!

2. **Believe It! BECOME IT!**
   Video Series: *Up Close and Personal with Paula Fellingham*

   From the comfort of your own living room you can enjoy Paula's *Believe It! BECOME IT!* presentation series. Paula mixes valuable, compelling content with delightful humor and enthusiasm as she reveals proven success strategies and shows you, step by step, how to overcome obstacles in your life—to hurdle barriers—and excel like you've never excelled before!

3. **Believe It! BECOME IT!**
   Audio Series: *Partner with Paula Fellingham*
   > Take Paula along with you and listen to ways the 5 Pillar Principles can transform you to become your ideal self. This audio series can absolutely change your life as Paula teaches how to go from where you are to where you want to be.

4. **Believe It! BECOME IT!**
   Personal Action Plan
   > A workbook that will be your key to success! It includes daily action items that lead you directly and speedily to goal achievement. The workbook assists you as you convert the *Believe It! BECOME IT!* principles into doable personal goals.

5. **Believe It! BECOME IT!**
   Words of Wisdom Booklet
   > 365 inspiring and uplifting quotes and short stories to keep you motivated and excited about your unlimited possibilities…every day of the year!

6. **FREE! Special Report:**
   "If You're Not Happy, Here's Why"
   > FREE to all who order! Paula discloses 5 reasons why people are unhappy, then she reveals 5 powerful, life-changing **solutions** that work.

Call today to receive this valuable program at a special low price offered only to "Believe It! Become It!" readers. Call 866.469.6636.

REFERENCES

Austin, L. (2000). *What's Holding You Back?* New York: Basic Books.

Brown, J., and K. Dutton. (1995). "The Thrill of Victory, the Complexity of Defeat: Self Esteem and People's Emotional Reaction to Success and Failure." *Journal of Personality and Social Psychology, 68*, 712.

Cassirer, N., and B. Reskin. (2000). "High Hopes: Organizational Position, Employment Experiences, and Women's and Men's Promotion Aspirations." *Work & Occupations, 27*, 438-63.

Chen, N. (1996). "Individual Differences in Answering the Four Questions for Happiness." Ph.D. dissertation, University of Georgia, Athens, Georgia.

Clark, F., M. Carlson, R. Zemke, F. Gelya, K. Patterson, and B. L. Ennevor. (1996). "Life Domains and Adaptive Strategies of a Group of Low Income, Well Older Adults." *American Journal of Occupational Therapy, 50*, 99.

Diener, E., and F. Fujita. (1995). "Resources, Personal Strivings, and Subjective Well-Being." *Journal of Personality and Social Psychology, 68*, 926.

Elliott, M. (1999). "Time, Work, and Meaning." Ph.D. dissertation, Pacifica Graduate Institute.

Frome, P. (1999). "The Influence of Girls' Gender-Linked Beliefs on Their Educational and Occupational Aspirations." Ph.D. dissertation, University of Michigan.

Garrett, R. (1996). "Wisdom as the Key to a Better World." In *Contemporary Issues in Behavior Therapy.* New York: Plenum.

Glass, J.C., and G. Jolly. (1997). "Satisfaction in Later Life." *Educational Gerentology, 23*, 297.

Gordone, Darlene. (1998). "The Relationship Among Academic Self-Concept, Academic Achievement, and Persistence with Self-Attribution." Ph.D. dissertation, Purdue University Press.

Hong, L., and R. Duff. (1997). "Relative Importance of Spouses, Children and Friends in the Life Satisfaction of Retirement Community Residents." *Journal of Clinical Geropsychology, 3,* 275.

Howatt, W.A. (1999). "Journaling to Self-Evaluation: A Tool for Adult Learners." *International Journal of Reality Therapy, 18,* 32-34.

King, L., and C. Napa. (1998). "What Makes a Life Good?" *Journal of Personality and Social Psychology, 75,* 156-65.

Lepper, H. (1996). "In Pursuit of Happiness and Satisfaction in Later Life: A Study of Competing Theories of Subjective Well-Being." Ph.D. diss., University of California, Riverside.

Lyubomirsky, S. (1994). "The Hedonistic Consequences of Social Comparison: Implications for Enduring Happiness and Transient Mood." Ph.D. diss., Stanford University, Palo Alto, California.

Maltz, Maxwell. (1993). *Psycho-Cybernetics.* Paramus, New Jersey: Prentice Hall.

Mendoza, J.C. (1999). "Resiliency Factors in High School Students at Risk for Academic Failure." Ph.D. dissertation, California School of Professional Psychology.

Murphy, Joseph (2000). *The Power of Your Subconscious Mind.* New York, New York: Reward Books.

Niven, David. *The 100 Simple Secrets of Successful People: What Scientists Have Learned and How You Can Use It.*

O'Brien, V., M. Martinez-Pons, and M. Kopala. (1999). "Mathematics Self-Efficacy, Ethnic Identity, Gender, and Career Interests Related to Mathematics and Science." *Journal of Educational Research, 92,* 231-35.

Parducci, A. (1995). *Happiness, Pleasure, and Judgment: The Contextual Theory and Its Applications.* Mahwah, NJ: Erlbaum.

Peale, Norman Vincent. (1952). *The Power of Positive Thinking.* Paramus, New Jersey: Prentice Hall.

Ricaurte, R.A. (1999). "Student Success in a Communicative Classroom: A Grounded Theory." Ph.D. dissertation, University of Nebraska.

Roberts, B., and W. Friend. (1998). "Career Momentum in Midlife Women." *Journal of Occupational Health Psychology, 3,* 195-208.

Schulman, P. (1999). "Applying Learned Optimism to Increase Sales Productivity." *Journal of Personal Selling and Sales Management, 19,* 31-37.

Scott, V.B., and W.D. McIntosh. (1999). "The Development of a Trait Measure of Ruminative Thought." *Personality & Individual Differences, 26,* 1045.

Sedlacek, W. (1999). "Black Students on White Campuses." *Journal of College Student Development, 40,* 538-50.

Sirgy, M.J., D. Cole, R. Kosenko, and H.L. Meadow. (1995). "A Life of Satisfaction Measure." *Social Indicators Research, 34,* 237.

Sommer, Bobbe. (2000). *Psycho-Cybernetics.* Paramus, New Jersey: Prentice Hall.

Sparrow, K.R. (1998). "Resiliency and Vulnerability in Girls During Cognitively Challenging Tasks." Ph.D. dissertation, Florida State University, Tallahassee.

Van Ekeren, Glenn. (1994). *Speaker's Sourcebook II,* Paramus, New Jersey: Prentice-Hall.

Velting, D. (1999). "Personality and Negative Expectations: Trait Structure of the Beck Hopelessness Scale." *Personality and Individual Differences, 26,* 913-21.

Williams, E., E. Soeprapto, K. Like, P. Touradiji, S. Hess, and C. Hill. (1998). "Perceptions of Serendipity." *Journal of Counseling Psychology, 45,* 379-89.

ABOUT THE AUTHOR

Bring Paula to your next convention or meeting and watch your newly-motivated group excel like never before!

Visit her website: www.BelieveitBecomeit.com, or email: paula@BelieveitBecomeit.com.

Call toll free: 877.U BELIEVE (823.5438) for information, or to request a speaker's package.

Paula has been an internationally-acclaimed goal achievement and relationship expert since 1987, speaking at the United Nations and at conferences across America and worldwide. A former radio show host and author of four books, Paula has reached many thousands with her message of how we can take immediate control of our thoughts, words and actions—creating positive change and excelling in every area of our lives. She offers proven strategies on how to overcome obstacles, increase joy and confidence, exceed goals—and much more—with her 5 Pillar Principles of Success. Her book and presentation, "Believe It! BECOME IT!" boosts morale, reveals specific ways to create positive change and reach goals, and inspires people to do their very best every day. Paula's presentation is content-rich, highly motivating, and absolutely delightful—with stories people want to hear and principles they can apply immediately. Paula Fellingham shows, step-by-step, how to hurdle barriers and excel like never before!